Rebecca Hood

Astrology
and
Tarot
For beginners

A Complete Guide to Discover the Secrets of Astrology and Tarot Reading

Copyright © 2020 publishing.

All rights reserved.

Author: Rebecca Hood

No part of this publication may be reproduced, distributed or transmitted in any form or by any means, including photocopying recording or other electronic or mechanical methods or by any information storage and retrieval system without the prior written permission of the publisher, except in the case of brief quotation embodies in critical reviews and certain other non-commercial uses permitted by copyright law.

Table of Contents

Types of Astrology 14

The Meaning Behind Astrology Symbols 20

Astrology and Mankind.. 24

Cornerstones of Astrology - Planets, Signs, Houses and Aspects 29

Astrology: A Science or Superstition? 40

Astrology System... 53

Charting the Basics of Astrology 56

Astrology for Beginners - Venus 62

How To Be A Professional Astrologer 71

Astrology Insights.. 74

Why Consider Astrology Now? 78

Astrology and the Renaissance 86

Helpful Advice On How To Learn Astrology 106

Vedic Astrology Helps Steer Key Life Decisions 111

What is Tarot? 116

Different Types of Tarot Packs 122

How Does Tarot Reading Work? 125

What is Paranormal Tarot Cards Reading? 131

Amateur Tarot Card Readings 134

Tarot Through the Ages 137

Steps To Giving a Great Tarot Reading 140

Things You Didn't Want to Know About Tarot 145

Tarot Cards for Beginners 157

RWS Tarot - A Brief Introduction 170

Waite Tarot - Information About Waite Tarot 173

Tarot Cards Spread 175

Tarot Myth Busters 179

Know All About Your Love Life Through Love Tarot Reading
.... 197

Traditional Tarot 220

Celtic Dragon Tarot 222

Tarot Symbolism and Meaning of the High Priestess Tarot Card
.... 232

Discover the Meaning of the Chariot Tarot Card 236

Rebecca Hood

Astrology

For beginners

A Complete Guide to Discover the Secrets of Astrology

The Truth About Astrology

It is said that astrology is the discipline that teaches us how to create horoscopes and use the positions of celestial bodies to understand and interpret human existence on Earth, at least what it says on a leading astrology website. I often encounter articles and comments that wonder if astrology is a science or trying to prove or disprove astrology in scientific terms. I do not see how an analogy can be drawn between astrology and modern science. Science and astrology are two very different disciplines, based on very different principles. Science follows the principles of experimentation, observation and inference; the scientific principles must have theoretical or mathematical evidence that must always be consistent. Although astrology has its own set of well-defined principles, they are very different from those of science.

Despite what many astrologers may claim, astrology is not without limits, and before we can proclaim Astrology One science or another, we must understand what these are. It is believed that astrology (Vedic) is the product of divine inspiration and was transmitted to the Hindu sage, 'Bhrigu' by the goddess of wealth, 'Mahalakshmi.' This knowledge was recorded in ancient sacred texts, of which only remains. Astrology is not a perfect discipline and is as good as the astrologer who practices it. Their competence determines the accuracy of the results and largely depends on their depth of knowledge, the type of experience (nature of the predictions made) and the duration of the experience. However, it would be logical to assume that even an astrologer, who is well-realized in all respects, cannot claim to have complete knowledge of astrology since his knowledge cannot go beyond the content of the texts still exist because the latter themselves are incomplete.

As explained on an astrology site, science and astrology are based on diametrically opposed views, as science always deals with exciting questions about the universe, the creation of the universe, the possibility of parallel universes, which minimizes a fraction of a second after the Big Bang and the beginning of time.

So, what was there before the beginning of time? If the universe has continued to expand since its creation, what does it extend into? Our knowledge is so limited that these questions seem absurd. Vedic astrology, on the other hand, comes from a belief system that is based on the principle that an explanation for everything that exists can be found in The Hindu scriptures or with their help. Many Vedic scholars believe that what scientists discover today was known to the sages all the time. For example, the twin Vedic planets, 'Rahu' and 'Ketu,' are unique to Vedic astrology. They are said to represent a mythical snake, with 'Rahu' as the head and 'Ketu' as the tail. These two planets are considered evil and devour other forms of energy, such as infinite wells and eclipse or weaken the sun and moon. The color of 'Rahu' is black and of 'Ketu' is grey. The similarity between 'Rahu' and 'Ketu' and black holes is quite surprising; the opposite end of a black hole is considered a white dwarf. Another case in question and also listed on the main astrology site mentioned above is the relevance of the number "108", which is the number of beads on a rosary of Hindu prayer beads. Although these prayer beads are a product of the ancient Vedic period, thanks to modern science, we now know that the figure "108" is of special importance since the distance between the Earth and the sun is about 108 times the diameter of the sun. The sun's diameter is about 108 times that of the Earth, and the distance between the Earth and the moon is about 108 times the diameter of the moon. Is it possible that the ancient Hindu sages could determine these celestial measurements, with such precision, long before the existence of telescopes?

Of course, none of the above proves anything scientifically, but wonders if science is really advanced enough to explain Astrology. In my opinion, to explain or unmask astrology, a scientist must first understand and have experience with the principles of astrology and must be able to practice astrology. I think he or she would understand that astrological predictions are not binary in nature, not everything is black and white, as in science, and there are authentic shades of gray.

In addition to being used to make predictions about the future, Vedic astrology also allows for corrective measures through the use of precious stones, talismans, prayer ceremonies, chants of mantras, etc.

According to the ancient Vedic scriptures, a parallel universe, complete with planets, stars, constellations, etc. exists in the human body. Obviously, this universe does not exist in the same physical form as we know from astronomy. However, its existence can be experienced by the awakening of the "kundalini", or "sleeping snake", a bright thread passing through the spinal cord, the awakening of which is the highest stage in "tantric" practices. Vedic astrology recognizes nine planets, twelve zodiacs and 28 constellations.

Pandit Sarvesh Nagar Vedic, the leading astrologer at the astrology site mentioned above, explains that the nine Vedic planets have obtained demigod status; however, these celestial bodies are not all-powerful and are based on offerings made on Earth for strength. When on Earth, we pray or apace the power that represents a planet, acquiring its precious stone or Yantra. We actually resort to the planet's power, present in our parallel universe. In this way, the planets are easily satisfied and respond by granting their blessings to their worshippers.

So, what does all this mean? Are there in heaven or in us the same powers that control our lives under Astrology? "As it is upstairs, it is also inside," seems to be the answer. Astrological influences are not distant objects that function in isolation; they are part of the universe of which we are also part, and we have the means to strengthen or appease them, as we wish. This does not mean that we can completely change fate; it would mean having the ability to change the position of the planets in our horoscopes, which is obviously impossible. What we need to remember is that despite Astrology, everyone is going through good and bad times. The basic principle of astrology is that actions are above the alarm, just like God, astrology helps those who help themselves, but using our knowledge of astrology, we can change the influences of the forces of the zodiac so that you can make the most of the good times and get the most out of them.

Types of Astrology

Astrology is the study of the relationship between the relative positions of some celestial bodies and life here on Earth. Because the word astrology comes from the Greek words astron, meaning 'star' and logos, meaning "word", we can literally translate astrology to mean the language of the stars; a language and practice that have developed over thousands of years by many cultures around the world from its first beginning recorded in the third millennium before the end of the century.

Indian or Jyotish, the foundation of Jyotisha, is based on the Sanskrit Bandhu of the Vedas, which describes the union between the inner and outer worlds. As with Western astrology, Jyotisha is based on the connection between the microcosm and the macrocosm. The microcosm is life on Earth, while the macrocosm is the universe.

The history of astrology

Although the terms astrology and astronomy have long been synonymous with each other, Astrology actually precedes astronomy and psychology. The oldest known astrological testimonies date back to Babylon in the distant 1645 BC. However, the history of astrology does not follow a particular timeline, but three independent branches that we call Western astrology, Indian or Jyotish astrology and Chinese or Eastern Asian astrology.

Chinese

Like Western and Indian astrology, it is believed that Chinese astrology originated in China in the third millennium. Similar to the hermetic law," as above, as below, "says Confucius" heaven sends its good or bad symbols. Astrology in China was then combined with Chinese practice known as Feng shui.

Western

It was believed that the study of Western astrology was first practiced among the ancient Babylonians in the third millennium BC. The Babylonians believed that the gods were responsible for all atmospheric phenomena, such as rain and sun. Egypt also has a very important place in astrological history. Star charts dating back to 4,200 BC show that Egypt has an ancient history with astrology. Pyramids are also oriented to the North Pole of the sky, as they served as astrological calculators, as well as burial places for astrological Pharaohs. In fact, Ramses II is often credited with fixing the positions of the cardinal signs Aries, Cancer, Libra and Capricorn. Some zodiac signs are also said to be of Egyptian origin, including Aries and Leo.

Houses and signs of the zodiac that remain practically unchanged today.

As Europeans became more literate, several periodicals and almanacs began to publish astrological information. Among the outstanding authors are Galileo and Copernicus, who practiced astrologers and founders of the modern scientific movement. However, the more popular astrology became, the more it was examined. And when the main astrological predictions did not come true, Astrology began to fall into disrepair.

It was only much later, with the birth of Princess Margaret in 1930, that astrology experienced a revival. To commemorate her birth, the British newspaper, London Sunday Express, published the princess's astrological profile, thus giving life to the newspaper's modern horoscope column.

Horoscope

Developed in Hellenistic Egypt, horoscopic astrology uses a visual representation of the heavens called horoscope, derived from the Greek word, horoskopos, which means "a look at the hours." This visual representation usually takes the form of a table or a diagram (below), which represents the positions of the sun, moon, planets, the astrological aspects, and angles at the time of a particular event, like the birth of a person.

Horoscope astrology is divided into four main branches of Christmas, worldly, elective and hourly.

1. Christmas astrology is the most commonly practiced form of horoscope astrology and is based on the idea that the personality or path of each individual in life can be determined by building a natal chart for the exact date, time and place of birth of a person.

2. Worldly astrology is one of the oldest forms of astrology and is named after the Roman word

Mundus, which means "the world."Worldly astrology is based on the idea that there is a correlation between individuals and world events, world affairs (wars, murders, etc.), and also geological phenomena such as earthquakes.

3. Election astrology is the practice of determining an individual's astrological profile to determine how and when to participate in a particular business or event, such as opening a business.

4. Hourly astrology is the practice in which the astrologer attempts to answer an individual's specific question by building a horoscope centered on that specific question. For example, "will I get a promotion at work?"

The Meaning Behind Astrology Symbols

The symbols of astrology are not the discovery of the century. People have known the symbols of astrology for many years. For many years, astrological symbols have been used to represent different zodiac signs. Once you have learned the meaning behind astrology symbols, you realize that they are easy to remember and recognize. The astrology symbols represent some signs of the zodiac so that the zodiac signs can be distinguished from each other.

Aquarius is considered the most discernible symbol of astrology. This symbol of astrology is always presented with figures, which resemble water. Someone can connect the waves in the image of the sign of astrology with an aquarium, but not with water. However, the astrology sign Aquarius is probably the easiest to remember.

Other astrological signs easy to remember are Taurus and Aries. The image of the astrological sign Taurus represents a Taurus. Its name can be easily remembered because the Spanish word for Taurus is the same. A sphere with two Taurus horns is usually the image of the sign of astrology Taurus. On the other hand, the astrology sign Aries is associated with a goat, and its image shows the horns on the head of a goat.

In the zodiac, there are two astrological symbols. That's why fish and twins often mix. Sometimes their images are quite similar. The figure of the astrological sign Pisces is usually presented with two Pisces. The image of the astrology sign of Pisces is always a pair of Pisces. The sign of astrology Gemini, on the other hand, is presented with an image reminiscent of the Roman Number II.

One of the most clearly recognized visual images of astrology symbols is that which represents the sign of astrology Leo. The mane of a lion or simply a lion is the symbol of the astrology of the lion.

Virgo and Scorpio are also quite similar astrological symbols. These two astrology symbols resemble the letter M. These remarkably different symbols of astrology are represented by icons, which are quite similar. The difference between the images is that the symbol of astrology Scorpio has a "tail" that adheres to the tip of an arrow outward. The "tail" of the Virgin is inward and has no arrow at its end.

Cancer and Sagittarius are two symbols of astrology, which are easy to distinguish. While the sign of cancer is quite feminine, the sign of Sagittarius is masculine. The astrology cancer symbol consists of two intersecting circles. The symbol of Sagittarius astrology is represented only by an arrow pointing up and to the right.

Capricorn is probably the strangest symbol of astrology. I don't know why, but their astrological symbol represents a goatfish. A goatfish is not the most pleasant picture possible, but I think the picture is not so bad. It looks like the lyrics vs

The last symbol of astrology, which remains, is Libra. This symbol of astrology resembles the scale of justice we see in the courts. They are usually associated with balance.

These symbols of astrology live for many generations and will probably expect many more to come.

Astrology and Mankind

American Heritage Dictionary defines Astrology as the study of the positions and aspects of celestial bodies in the belief that they influence the course of natural earthly events and human affairs. Planetary observation is the basis of astrology. The practice of astrology was widespread even in ancient times.

The history of astrology is an important part of civilization and goes back to the early days of the human race. Some of the world's known civilizations have widely used this field. For example, the ancient Chinese civilization, the Egyptian civilization, the ancient Indian civilization, etc., all astrology practiced at one time or another. Arabs also practiced astrology before the advent of Islam. The Arabs were quite advanced in the field of Astronomy.

The ancient Babylonians were probably the first to use astrology. The Babylonians were the first to name the days of the week after the sun, moon, and planets. They were also the first to define the twelve houses of the zodiac. Baghdad and Damascus were known as centers of astrology and Astronomy in ancient times. Egypt contributed greatly to the development of astrology. It is believed that some of the astrological signs of the zodiac originated in Egypt.

The Greek astronomer Ptolemy was the first person to write a book on astrology. He codified the astrology of the Sun sign we know today. Ptolemy tried to predict the positions of celestial bodies between themselves and the Earth by knowing their orbital movements. During its time, astrology was part of astronomy. Later, astronomy became an exact science, and astrology remained part of theology.

Chinese astrology insists on the five elements, metal, wood, water, fire and Earth. The zodiac signs used by them are also different from other forms of astrology.

India has a rich history of astrology. Astrology was practiced even in Vedic times in India. Astrology is one of the six disciplines of Vedanga. Even the ancient Hindu scriptures attach great importance to the various aspects of planetary movements and their effects on humans. Astrology is still studied and practiced by many in India.

It is considered vital in Indian culture. It is used to make decisions about marriage, start new businesses and move to a new home, etc. Hindus believe that human luck or unhappiness in life is due to karma, and the movements of the planets must influence karma. Among Hindus, the Brahmins are considered the best authorities in astrology.

Astrologers in India argue that this is a scientific method for predicting the future. They still have clubs in this field of study in the parameters of Hinduism. Hindus almost unanimously believe in astrological predictions. In fact, religious Hindus cannot imagine life without Astrology. More and more Indians began to build their homes according to the principles of Vastu Shashtra.

This ancient Indian tradition is also governed by astrological implications. Hindus believe that the occupants' general prosperity and benefits depend on the principles of Vastu when building the house. Indian astrologers claim that they can prove that astrological predictions are really scientific.

Horoscope is a part of astrology. Daily horoscope reading has become a trend, even in the developed countries of the West. The Western mind has always put any subject under scrutiny and tends to rely solely on scientific facts.

But this does not prevent Westerners from obsessing over their horoscopes. Suddenly, the Western world realized the possibility of knowing and improving its future using astrology. More and more Westerners began to believe in the possibility of being hit by powerful planets and stars.

Western researchers have included the subject of astrology in their research. Astrology has never been examined and studied before as it has in recent years. In this regard, Indian astrologers must present themselves and show the world the power of astrology.

Cornerstones of Astrology - Planets, Signs, Houses and Aspects

Reading the charts is the unconscious goal of all who study astrology, even if they do not realize it. You can take any beginner book or astrological Journal and read what others have written about the different parts of astrology. What he wants to achieve most personally is the ability to look behind the wheel and decipher what he says and what it means. This requires personal effort, good memory and time.

Astrology Sun sign is very popular and is considered the daily, weekly or monthly mini-readings made for the twelve signs. I wrote a lot of columns for magazines and newspapers, as well as radio and television programs. A real effort is needed to transform these simple sentences, especially those with which you identify closely. You can't just take sentences off the air, or you shouldn't because some readers or listeners literally take what you say. I often thought someone followed me, to be precise. Other times, it's like the column speaks a foreign language that has nothing to do with me. Accuracy has to do with the astrologer's skill and the receptivity of the audience.

Astrology Sun sign is very generic in nature. The equivalent of a prayer addressed to 1/12 of the world's population has to connect with someone, doesn't it? Most people know their Sun sign to know which prayer to read. If you know your ascending sign, you can get twice the column's mileage and you will somehow identify yourself with these phrases. Add your moon sign, and you can get a little smaller piece from this column. I doubt that even well-written and accurate solar panel columns can give much more to the man on the street who has a superficial understanding of solar panels. Astrology Sun sign is very generic but very popular and easily accessible, but it is a shortened version of real astrology.

So, what is true about astrology? It is a map of the sky built for an individual using the date, time and place of birth (longitude and latitude in the world). Since two births cannot occupy the same space simultaneously, that moment creates a map for an individual. (We pushed this particular envelope with multiple births, didn't we? However, my brother is married to a twin, and the Twins are very different.) This map of the moving sky provides the astrologer with a diagram of possibilities and intention for this individual that can be seen and read as a moving dynamic. Reading the chart is the reason you go to an astrologer and is also the way you, yourself, could get infected with the error of astrology, so you can do this reading by yourself. Having existed for many years and having studied many self-help techniques, astrology is undoubtedly the best technique I have found to understand myself and my life. Once you get a sample of what you can do for you, you want more, even if you have to work to get more.

When you look at a map of the sky that is yours, a map just about you and your life, the sky is really the limit. All kinds of new doors also open the first door of the sun sign that you can read in your local newspaper. There are other bodies besides the sun, which are collectively called planets. I know, I know. The sun is not a planet; it is a star. The moon is not a planet; it is a satellite of the Earth. It is easier to tell the planets collectively than The Sun, Moon and planets. Repeat after me "ease of reference, ease of reference."

So, we have the 12 Sun Signs (You need to learn them all, not just your Sun sign) and planets, which greatly expanded what we initially needed to study. If you look at the wheel provided when you launch your Sky Map, you will see 12 wheel segments like the orange or grapefruit segments contained with the fruit balloon. The wheel represents the wheel of life. It's the land we're all on, earth to earth, physical reality, all that. Since all of this at once is difficult to understand, we conveniently divide it into smaller segments called houses. The whole wheel represents the individual's whole life, and the 12 divisions represent segments of that life, or what I call sands of interest. There is a segment for your physical body and yourself. There's a segment for your parents and family. There is a segment for your profession and career, and so on. Each division covers about 1/12 of its size, so it is very small, the compartments are full of problems. Add this to what you need to understand to make a reading. We now have three categories, with a lot of work, but it is an important category.

Aspects are the most intense area of astrology learning. Why is that? The aspects should assume that you already know the planets, the signs and the houses because now you have to make them interact or form relationships. Aspects are no longer difficult as a topic, but you need the other three categories of work before making sense and knowing how to apply aspects in a reading.

If I were suggesting a study guide, I would suggest solar signs as a good place to start reading because we already have an advantage with the popularity of astrology Sun sign. Just know that this is only a thin first layer. Here you will begin to learn the nature of signs, a prerequisite for the application of planets in these signs. There are 12 signs, but there are many combinations to learn in these signs, such as cardinal, fixed and mutable, fire, earth, air and water, symbols or glyphs, myths, etc.

The ten bodies we collectively call the planets would be my next suggestion to study because the planets will become more and more important as they develop their astrological ability. Study them one at a time and in-depth because each represents a guiding principle, influence or energy in relation to life.

Then he studies astrological houses in all their glory. Each house represents 1/12 of your life experience, so every small house is full of problems and events. There's really a lot to learn, so take your time. You have your life to follow this study.

Last but not least, to study the aspects. As mentioned, the combination represented by the angular relationship between two bodies or points requires you to understand the two bodies or points individually before studying the relationship formed between them. Aspects can get into your face and require your attention. Signs and houses will also enter this act, so study the aspects once you have learned the language of the other three categories. This is your basic study guide, the order in which to study the four categories.

Now I have to change the speed in terms of the order of importance in the application or reading. My best analogy for a beginner student is to think about building a house. First of all, the country, city, district, subdivision, lot, architectural plans and the builder, all the necessary preliminary works are selected. Astrologically chooses the type of astrology, Eastern or Western (sidereal or tropical), geocentric or heliocentric, graphic and wheel type, defines its goal: all preliminary stages leading to the configuration of the map of the sky itself. All this brings us to the equivalent of laying the foundation of the house. At this stage, the wheel may look like a spaghetti dish that needs to be fixed and deciphered.

Usually, after placing the base, the cornerstones are placed. In our analogy, the building now has a guide or dimension to the natural flow of what is to come. Astrologically cornerstones are planets, signs, houses and aspects. Once your wheel is configured and visible, you will move on to the four categories mentioned above to understand this map of the sky and use the information generated by your study of the four categories to read or translate it. As long as you have a plan and work on the plan, you will be amazed at how much information you can get from this sky map. This wonderful set of information will constantly increase as you develop your knowledge and skills through experience. The first time I wrote a table read, I generated over a dozen pages of information about a total stranger. He was dumb founded; the stranger was dumbfounded. He had also clung. It was 36 years ago, and I still do Astrology.

We have four cornerstones that should be studied diligently, and thanks to this study, we developed a set of information about each. One of these cornerstones must become the cornerstone, which drives or controls the flow of information for this graph. The order I gave them to study now must change as the natural key category progresses. The cornerstone is the planets. Planets "regulate" signs and houses. You will discover aspects (angular relationships) that may seem very similar to the nature of some planets.

Most of what we can learn and apply can be defined as what, where, when, why and how of existence. We can determine what, where, why and how through these four birth categories.

- What about our lives, as principles, energies, impulses and motivations, are planets

- The place of our lives, such as topics, events, the arena of interest are the houses
- How our lives, such as attitudes, expressions, gestures or coloring, are the signs.
- Why our lives such as stress, conflict, luck, flow or constriction are the aspects
- When is a native and dynamic personal graphic function

It's very easy. Once you learn the basic principles of the four categories, the rest is application and experience. Your skill develops naturally and sequentially. There is always more to study, but the development of an organized body of information that you have taken the time to consolidate in your consciousness is what provides the basis for everything you can and will do. If you skimp on studying these categories, you'll have a weak, porous base, holes in your knowledge that can stumble every time until you fill those empty spaces in your astrological skill toolkit. I know because I've been there and I've done this. These four categories are the place for you to start building a solid foundation of astrological knowledge that will find no end to apply to your life. If I regret anything about my astrological studies, it is that I have not started before. Previously, I would have made my life more understandable, especially during the most difficult episodes.

Enjoy your meal. A heterogeneous virtual astrological mix awaits you, limited only by the limits you place or allow them to be placed there. The universe (and its Creator) provided us with a giant map of potential and possibility and gave us enough brains to develop the ability to read it. Go to him!

Astrology: A Science or Superstition?

Humans have always been curious about their future. Whenever someone is in trouble and can not easily get out of it, he wants to know if the days of his misery will end. And, if so, when? When a lot of time, effort or money is invested in a project, it is natural to wonder if this investment will pay off. There have always been people around who have successfully predicted future events. Their methods were different: some people can look to the future, some use Tarot cards, some draw up an astrological card that we call horoscopes, some read lines on people's palms. It cannot be denied that the future has been accurately predicted many times and by many people. Each successful prediction shows that it is really possible to predict the future correctly.

In ancient times, astrologers were highly esteemed by people. There was no difference between astronomers and astrologers. In fact, astronomy and astrology were not considered two different topics. Many will be surprised to learn that most of the past renowned scientists, including Sir Isaac Newton, were also astrologers. In ancient India, astrology was known as "Jyotish Shastra", which included predictive astrology and what we know as astronomy. Needless to say, the astrologers of that time were also great mathematicians. A consummate astrologer was called "Trikal-darshee": the one who could see the past, the present and the future. Perhaps it would not be an exaggeration to say that astrology was considered the most important branch of science.

Slowly, over some time, this issue has fallen into disrepute.

How does astrology lose its exalted status?

It is a fact of life that people imitate successful, popular and respected people. Seeing the social status enjoyed by astrologers, The Charlatans began to disguise themselves as astrologers. They learned some tricks of the trade and began to deceive gullible people. It was and remained a very profitable business. An astrologer makes money making predictions, with no guarantee that any of his predictions will turn out to be true. There is no money-back guarantee. Once an astrologer creates a shop, people begin to turn to him, hoping that he can correctly predict his future. The astrologer is in a wonderful position. For example, you can make predictions on ten people, getting only one correct prediction. The nine people, whom he mistakenly predicted, will never return to him. But the tenth person, whose astrologer could correctly predict, will not only return to him but will also return many other people, citing personal experience. In this way, an astrologer's activity always flourishes, no matter how much he enters his profession. But the disadvantage of this was that astrologers, as a group, began to consider many dubious people as politicians of the modern era. Once such an impression began to gain ground, astrology as a topic was no longer attractive to intelligent people. People who had talent began to pursue other areas of knowledge. Over a period of time, the inevitable happened. No talent worth his salt chose to pursue astrology as a vocation or a hobby, and the result of this is for everyone to see it in the present times.

There was another very important reason why astrology became one of the minor areas of knowledge. It was the decline of India, the source of human civilization, and its loss of the status of the depositary of all knowledge of the ancient world (see how India lost its glory). The Islamic hordes, who attacked and plundered India several times and then ruled that country for hundreds of years, had no respect for priceless works of art, magnificent architecture and other exalted areas of human effort. They destroyed most of the ancient temples, burned libraries like Nalanda and Takshshila, and definitely brought countless books of infinite wisdom to future generations of mankind. A lot of recorded knowledge, including astrological books, was lost. This loss was irreparable, as Indian society at that time was committed to ensuring its survival and a constant fight against the aggressors. The few people, who had with them invaluable texts and scriptures, were difficult to preserve the remaining works of the ancient sages. That's why, when studying astrology, it seems that some vital links are missing. With Hindu philosophy losing its ground, it was natural that astrology would lose its prominent place as well. As modern science developed and the scientific temperament gained ground, Astrology began to fade into oblivion with the shortage of real astrologers.

Criticism and advocacy

Astrology is mocked by people for two main reasons. First, of course, is that predictions made by astrologers often go wrong. Second, if one brings his horoscope to different astrologers, they make different predictions. They also make different horoscopes given the same set of data relating to a person's birth. These facts force people to conclude that astrology is not a science and is just a way to cool people for the benefit of astrologers.

It cannot be denied that the above reasons are valid. However, there is an element of prejudice against astrology that also plays a role in the denigration of this science. Let us give an example to illustrate this point.

A man gets sick because of an illness. He's going to see his local doctor. The doctor advises him to take tests. After seeing the results of these tests and taking into account the patient's symptoms, the doctor concludes that the man has contracted a particular disease, for example, the disease: -). He prescribes certain medications, and the patient returns home, hoping to get rid of the disease as soon as possible. After taking the medications for the next two days, the patient discovers that the medications do not work as they should. He goes back to the doctor, and the doctor changes the medications, and the person immediately begins to respond to the second set of medications. Within a few days, the person returned to his old healthy self.

What would have happened if the person had not responded to this second set of medications? Most likely, he would have gone to another doctor. This doctor would have advised him to take other tests, diagnosed his problem based on his knowledge and experience and treated him accordingly. Again, there would have been the same probability that the patient would get rid of his illness.

So, in the end, it boils down to the problem of the correct diagnosis. As soon as the disease is correctly identified, it can be successfully treated. The doctor's problem is to correctly identify the disease, taking into account the symptoms and the results of the tests performed. In fact, he guesses the disease according to the symptoms shown by the patient and to confirm his suspicions; the doctor asks the patient to undergo a particular series of tests. If the doctor's first hypothesis is incorrect, he suggests to the patient another series of tests aimed at confirming his second-best hypothesis of the disease.

There is another element that can ruin the patient's chances of improving: the test results. If the laboratory that performs these tests makes a mistake, the doctor is bound to be deceived by the results. It has also been repeatedly observed that even with the same symptoms and the same set of test results, different doctors can diagnose the problem differently.

When it happens in the context of astrology, the same thing is offered as evidence that this is not a science. When a doctor makes a mistake, his skills are not attributed to medical science. But if an astrologer fails, it is astrology that is considered pseudoscience. If doctors can come to different conclusions based on the same data, why should astrologers not be allowed to differ from each other? If you take blood samples from the same patient in different laboratories, you will almost certainly find differences in your results. If machines built with all our scientific knowledge at our disposal make mistakes, no one denigrates modern science. But when it comes to astrology, people are too willing to reject it. Perhaps, by doing this, people want to prove that they have, so-called scientific temperament.

Why are astrologers mistaken in their predictions?

Lack of knowledge - this is perhaps the main reason. Having learned a little, most astrologers find it difficult to resist the temptation to start making predictions. A certain percentage of their predictions turn out to be true because they learned a little bit of astrology, after all. They can not help but show their half-baked knowledge. Another reason is the temptation to start reaping, as soon as possible, the fruits of their efforts to learn the topic. Once customers start turning to them, they lose momentum to continue learning more. In addition, they have little free time to make more effort to learn more. They're too busy fooling people.

Lack of talent: in modern times, since the search for this topic is not considered very respectable; genius people do not take the study of astrology. They prefer to become scientists, engineers, doctors, literati, artists, etc. this does not help the development of astrology, nor does it help to add knowledge or find the missing links in this topic.

Currently, there are no serious research projects related to this area. Therefore, this knowledge base is not updated.

Incorrect data: since the very basis of astrology is mathematics, data such as time of birth, etc., you need to be specific. If these data are incorrect, the horoscope, and, accordingly, the interpretation of it is bound to be defective. The location of the cusps, the divisions of the houses and the planetary positions at a given time must also be accurate. The many ephemerides differ so much from each other that it seems incredible. You need to follow the most accurate data (for example, from NASA) for calculations in this era of science. Typically, astrologers tend to take the easy road, follow some kind of things ready to prove, leading to inaccuracies in their calculations.

Fate of the subject: it may happen that the fate of the person who wants to read his future does not favor the person to know his future. This idea may sound crazy, but it is not. Even in modern times, with all medical science development, patients continue to die from curable diseases. If a person is destined to die from pneumonia, he will do this despite the fact that millions of people around the world receive successful treatment every year. Fate can play a role here, but it can not play the same role as astrology.

The very nature of the future: modern science divides the universe into two parts, known and unknown. He believes that everything that is unknown today will be published tomorrow. For a while, everything will be known one day. But enlightened sages said that some aspects of existence are unknowable. These things do not belong to the realm of human knowledge. Some aspects of the future belong to the same domain.

Anyone, who will study astrology with an open mind, can not reject it as something without merit. It is an easy task for astrologers to accurately say certain things about a man, such as his physical characteristics, the diseases that are likely to be afflicted, his temperament, his general success in life in terms of the money he earns or the fame he achieves, the nature of your profession, etc. simply by looking at your horoscope is correctly drawn. It is in the details and timing of events that astrologers tend to be mistaken. What is needed is a new approach to the issue. Bright minds need to take it for study, correct some anomalies and misconceptions that this science has acquired in the past. Thus, only this subject can regain its rightful place as a serious and important branch of knowledge.

Astrology System

Astrology is the combination of beliefs, systems and traditions that can provide future information about human personality, earthly matter and human relationships. The person who practices this astrology is called an astrologer. Most astrologers believe that nature and natural things have an influence on the body and human behavior. They believe that nature has a direct or indirect influence on humans.

If desired, you should most often consider a symbolic language, or it is an art form, or it is the form of divination. It has so many definitions. Different astrologers gave different definitions, but every astrologer believes in one thing that can explain the present, past and future.

Astrology is considered totally incorrect by the scientific community. The scientific community called it superstitions, but the psychological community explains it positively. Some people say that astrology is related to science.

Astrology has a great history. Since ancient times, people of the world have practiced this thing. Before 3000 BC, people practiced it, which is recorded. It plays an important role in the formation of World culture. Astrology has a relationship with astronomy, Vedas and various types of historical incidents.

A few centuries ago, astrology and astronomy were considered the same. After the eighteenth century, when the Renaissance began, Astrology separated from astronomy. Even now, the astrologer relies on astronomy to analyze Astrology. Some astrologers still think that astrology is apart of astronomy.

The word astrology comes from the Latin term "Astrology"(Astronomy). It was derived from the Greek word "Astron" (star) and "Logia," meaning study. So, the study of the star is Astrology. From the history of astrology, we can easily understand that it is related to astronomy.

Most astrological things are based on the movement of stars and the planet. Planets are signed by certain symbols. Astrology also shows the geometric and angular relationship between different types of planets and events. This question define all kinds of human nature and accidents.

According to Western tradition, predictive Astrology explains two methods: astrological transits and astrological progressions. The method of astrological transits explains the movement of the planets. In the astrological progression method, the horoscope progresses according to the established method.

In the past, the astrologer observed only celestial bodies and their movement, but today the peoples of the world have made great progress in this area. Although there is great controversy about astrology, some people still believe in it and try to follow the rules of astrology. Then it's up to a person how he's going to take this.

Charting the Basics of Astrology

Do you know the basics of astrology? Astrology is one of those ancient "sciences" that many people are still fascinated with, but they do not know much more about which page of the local newspaper their horoscope will appear. So, what are the basics of astrology?

In this article, we'll take a look at some of the things you need to know about astrology. First of all, let's look at what it is and where it is suspected to come from. So, let's look at what forms the astrological chart. Finally, we will look at astrology and horoscope.

The basics of astrology: in the beginning...

It is said that astrology reaches as far as the Babylonians in the second millennium BC, making it by far one of the oldest "sciences."The word "astrology" has the same Latin root (astrology) as" astronomy", although the two are now considered completely different in terms of scientific validity. However, in the early days, it will be considered in the opposite direction, with astrology having a strong connection with religion.

What makes an astrological chart?

An astrological chart is a way of tracing planets and includes the sun and the moon, but it does not include the Earth because it is the point from which we see the other planets.

The picture is divided into twelve "houses";each house represents one aspect of life. The houses are (in Latin and translation): Vita (life), Lucrum (wealth), Fratres (brothers), father (parent), Nati (children), Valetudo (health), uxor (spouse), Mors (death), ITER (travels), Regnum (Kingdom), Benefacta (friendship) and Carcer (prison).

Eagle eyes of you may have noticed that ten planets and twelve houses leave two empty houses, but fear not, both empty houses are considered areas of your life that have been mastered-in a different life.

The first thing studied on an astrology table is the sign of the sun, which is determined by the position of the sun. The positions of the planets are studied depending on the influence they have on the Sun sign. The moon sign is the last to be studied according to how it relates to other planets on the astrological chart.

The most common astrological chart (in the first days) was the theme of birth. The birth theme was used to show what the person's personality would look like. A natal chart may be established for someone later in their life, but it may seem not to resemble the person - this is said to be due to the fact that other events will alter a person's personality over time.

Where does the astrology and horoscope link come from in all this?

To begin with, the twelve signs of the zodiac were related to the twelve astrological houses: Aries (Vita), Taurus (Lucrum), Gemini (Fratres), cancer (spawner), Lion (Nati), Virgo (Valetudo), Libra (Uxor), Scorpio (Mors), Sagittarius (ITER), Capricorn (Regnum), Aquarius (Benefacta) and Pisces (Carcer).

This mixture of astrology and horoscope (Horoscope Astrology) would have begun in the Mediterranean at the end of the second or early I century BC. The horoscope is a visual illustration of the sky and is used to interpret the meaning of the alignment of planets at this time in time.

What makes it different from other forms of astrology is that it is more complex and includes other factors such as "the ascendant," which is the degree of the eastern horizon when it rises in the elliptical background. However, this goes beyond the definition of "basics of astrology."

That is, a horoscope is more than a minute after minute, the version of the Natal astrologer and allows the current positions of celestial bodies, while the Natal astrologer is routed into the positions at the time of birth.

Here we have the basics of astrology. Of course, we could have had a lot more depth on the whole subject and started to cover interpretations, etc.

but you need to know where you are to understand where you are going.

We have seen that astrology, which is the first in the horoscope, we have found that astrology is based mainly on someone's birth(or something more) and is used to show how you will develop in the future; however, a Christmas gift by an elderly person may not correspond to the person, because of the other, and then, finally, we have seen that the horoscope is essentially a way to adapt the graphic concept, integrating other factors, give an updated version of their astrological chart.

Astrology for Beginners - Venus

Let's look at the "goddess of love"—Venus and see what she brings when she enters each house. Transits are also like a "weather forecast" covering everything and everyone connected to the house who still visit; we all respond differently. Keep things simple when a planet enters every house.

Venus the first: it's time to spoil one way or another. It's time to seriously think about your values, review the past year and see whether your sense of value has increased or decreased. Depending on which natal planets you have on the first, Look for conjunctions because Venus will encourage you to work harder or make you lazy in perspective.

To take an example: Venus spouse your Christmas. Venus could mean the beginning of a romance! Holidays, good friends and happy moments are the order of the day; enjoy them. It's time to appreciate yourself and stop worrying about others. Avoid extravagance and seriously think about preparing a "budget" for the coming year...

Venus in the second: you may find yourself starting a new romance right now. You want to buy nice things, you want to party, make new friends and happy moments are the order of the day now, enjoy them for you need to have fun and have a good time. As Venus moves through this sector, they focus on income, earnings, expenses and savings, values and their understanding of love...

Venus in the third: you will have an appreciation of intellectual beauty, and it will be easy to discuss your feelings with someone without feeling embarrassed. You might even find yourself telling someone that you love them or talking with friends about your love life more freely. Your words will have a tingling of love or passion, passing through them—use it to your advantage. You will also begin to recognize the "beauty" that surrounds you, and relationships with women, in general, bring rewards that have lasting effects.

Venus in the fourth: you will feel that others are for or against you: this transit is not lasting, to minimize unnecessary conflict, to ten before entering into any kind of discussion with your loved ones! Friends, family, parents or children will make you feel a little emotional (crying for no apparent reason). If you feel restless and moody, go out and visit places of interest or invite friends.

Venus in the fifth: you do not want to be alone at this time, and if your relationships go well, everything will be fine. If there are problems, they can or will arise! You will have the power to attract the opposite or the same sex, so "alurve" is in the air, and if you are interested or available, a new love interest may appear on the horizon —go out and socialize, make new friends and Party, Party, Party!!! Money and new goods, as well as new friends or lovers (he could be on your side). This is a good transit for all financial activities, as long as you are not extravagant in order to use common sense and a little restriction. This should be a nice time, do not sit and wait for things to happen, go out and have fun!

Venus in the sixth: this is a good position for health unless you abuse your body for self-indulgence and rich and sweet foods. You should avoid excess sugar and starches. Romance and gossip about romance in the workplace abound at this time. Your thoughts become real during this transit, so thinking and acting positively can be home for the health. Remember the word exaggeration in all areas of life, and prioritize your daily routine: take into consideration the best diet health! On the job front, for too small, conversations interferes with the work that leads to gossip, and if you are looking for a raise or waiting for a promotion, this will happen if you are ready and have prepared the way! Remember, if you beat him on the "promotion poles," he was not ready.

Transit to Venus in 7: you can find yourself starting a new romance right now for the holidays; good friends and happy moments are the order of the day. You should have fun and have fun. Do not be too extravagant, brag or be too greedy for fun, and if you have the need to buy beautiful things think in terms of needs you do not want! Think twice about the purchases you make for yourself and your family because it may be tasteless or too expensive. Whether it's a man or a woman, there could be relationship problems with women or your partner! Think positive, be positive, and remember, this is the House Of Attraction, and like a magnet being a magnet, you can not do without attracting iron...

Venus in 8: this will prove to be a very intense period in which to delve into relationship problems or create something in a relationship that is not really there! Create problems if you are currently in a relationship—want more "intensity" than your partner might be able to give. Don't be jealous or manipulative! As this transit unfolds, you will discover a new you (good or bad, positive or negative, this is the question of $ 60,000). You will feel more lustful or, beware of others who are sexually powerful! Think twice before accepting unusual gifts: keep the property and financial affairs of scammers! Note that this is the home of radical change and fundamental with other people's money: the banks, construction companies, credit unions, or the old "uncle Frank" during this transit, try not to listen to the negativity of others.

Transit to Venus in 9: this is a good time to enjoy more music and romance, you should also be lucky with money! Many celebrations will come your way to make the most of the Times that await us and enjoy the festive atmosphere. Lucky lady is around to look for your favors! Travel to foreign places, whether for a long or short stay, raise spirits, talk about such, there will be greater communication with the higher realms, spiritual realms, and an epiphany is also possible during this period! The future must appear and feel brighter than it has been for some time...

Venus on day 10: you will feel a little bit calm and sober during this transit, even saying "goodbye" to a loved one or, on the contrary, meeting someone who will become a friend or lover for life. If you feel lonely or have problems with someone you love, do not be afraid to talk about your feelings, and sexual inhibition could make you feel more frustrated than usual, build bridges, not walls! Loyalty and self-control, especially with older members of your family, will give you a lot of inner pleasure. You risk becoming more conservative in your financial affairs; this is a good time to establish a business or partnership that will lead to lasting success. On another level, you may be seriously interested in music, art, or antiques.

The transit of Venus in the 11 unexpected things happen, in old and new relationships you can win or lose in everything you undertake, so take a chance, because it will make you wiser and somehow much richer. You will experience oddities in your love life, letting your emotions go to extremes; there will be mood swings and a desire for greater independence! Children or people younger than you can get on your nerves now, so don't say the things you may regret later. A new romance can be in the air, people are more exciting, life is more interesting, and you have more freedom to do your own thing. Be careful not to become too enamored or too excited!

Venus on the 12th: during this transit of the 12th, you are in a dreamlike world, so wait for it to pass by to make a judgment or to make real decisions. For the moment, try to enjoy anything of beauty, travel or listen to the little secrets of others. Pay attention to financial or romantic deception at this time because it is known that this transit comes out of the closet to any secret admirer. You are very impressionable now, and if alone or feeling a little lonely, you might be attracted to a false and deceived sense of love, prevented is saved! Love is not what it seems now. Relax a little more mentally, and when negative thoughts appear in your mind, do not connect or kiss them; otherwise, you may be on the verge of a nervous breakdown! You can also be invited to travel to beautiful places where a new platonic love can appear, which brings you a lot of fun and a new breath in life.

How To Be A Professional Astrologer

A professional astrologer has many obstacles on the way to the demonstration activity of professional astrological consultations. There are no companies that hire professional astrologers; it is a company that will need entrepreneurial skills with superior astrological knowledge.

Usually, you do not choose to be an astrologer; the profession calls you. It's really a vocation. A future astrologer is forced to share mysteries and messages from the universe to help others with a system that provides so much wisdom and understanding.

Excellent training is essential to pave the way for a good astrologer. There are several professional organizations that offer lessons that will give you access to the world's best and famous astrologers.

For Continuing Education, find a local Astrology group or organization that has monthly or bimonthly meetings. Many local astrological groups will also have Astrology lessons for beginners and intermediates. There are professional Astrology certification courses offered by National Astrology organizations that will measure your level of learning. Kepler college offers a bachelor's and a master's degree in astrology.

If you do not have a local Astrology club, sign up for online courses and go to regional conferences. Once you are introduced to the different disciplines of astrology, you want to reduce your attention to an astrological field that suits your temperament. You can be subject to psychological, predictive, financial, hourly, cosmobiology, Vedic astrology, to name a few.

Reading is essential. There are hundreds of books that will help you understand more deeply how to interpret a graph. It is recommended to choose authors who practice the type of astrology that interests you. Once you've learned your art, start by providing astrology letter readings to your friends to get feedback. Feedback on your skills is essential to hone your knowledge of the book.

Being a professional astrologer is a rewarding experience; knowing that you help others understand their destiny and their path in life through astrology brings satisfaction. Professional astrological consultations can help others at different times of crisis and in normal times to determine what planetary influences are around a person.

If you feel the call to be a professional astrologer, be patient with the process. Getting different personal readings from other astrologers will give you an idea of the different styles of astrological readings and help you know what you need to do to become a good astrologer. Use the messages on your astrology chart to help you on your way to becoming a professional Astrology consultant.

Astrology Insights

Astrology is an extremely ancient and diverse discipline and cannot be dealt with in detail here. The purpose of this summary is to provide an understanding of some basic concepts and ultimately incorporate your desire to learn more. There are great books for beginners available that do a great job of putting astrology in easily understandable terms. In the past, most of the books available were too technical and difficult to decipher.

Three information is needed if an astrologer is going to draw a picture for you: where you were born, your date of birth, and, if possible, the time of your birth. If you do not have your own time of birth, the astrologer will still be able to create a chart, but it will not be so detailed. The astrologer will draw up a table based on the position of the planets when you were born. From this image, they can tell you what you can expect in your life, how your childhood was, what talents you possess, the negative aspects of yourself you have overcome and your positive traits. You can also, if you want, what you have achieved in this life.

If you have rebates on your board, and most people have at least one, it means that you have not learned some lessons in one or more previous lives and have tried again. For example, let's say that Mercury, the planet that governs communication, is retrograde on its map. This means that in a previous life, you misinterpreted something important through the spoken or written word. Maybe you taught bad information or wrote books that were seriously flawed in the information they gave. If this is the case, you will probably find in this life that you have difficulty communicating. One of my clients with retrograde Mercury has dyslexia, another has difficulty communicating vocally, and another has difficulty writing.

A Christmas theme has planets, signs and houses. There are ten planets used in astrology, and the ten are found in each natal chart. The astrological sign that contains each house and each planet differs with each person, but these planets affect us all. The ten planets are The Sun, Moon, Mercury, Mars, Venus, Jupiter, Saturn, Neptune, Uranus and Pluto (despite their recent scientific degradation). They represent the ten fundamental and different ways in which we express ourselves, negatively or positively, and when this information is combined with the information represented by signs and houses, a detailed description of a person arises.

If you want to learn more, there are a multitude of ways to do it —there are several books, as I said, there is the internet and its wealth of information, there are workshops (I teach personally - see the link to the right), and so on. I generally suggest reading books about the signs of the sun as a good starting point. Once you have learned about the signs of the sun, you can proceed to read the signs of the Moon, then Mercury, Mars, Venus, Jupiter, Saturn, Uranus, Neptune and Pluto. If you take one step at a time, you will find that astrology is a wonderful discipline to learn, not only as an object but also as a tool to help you understand yourself. Once you do this, you can start getting to know others around you and understand why they are the way they are.

Why Consider Astrology Now?

Astrology is the method for determining a person's character and future through the alignment of stars and planets. Astrology does not work and cannot predict future events or personalities. Eastern astrology is event-oriented. They will tell you what happened in the past and what will happen in the future much more accurately. The most widespread application of the astrology horoscope is to use it to analyze the birth charts of individuals in order to read character, psychological traits and, to some extent, Destiny.

Astrology of the Arab era is the immediate ancestor of Western astrology today. Our astrology may, in fact, be the successor to the third current of ancient astrology. Developed by the Greeks and based on some of the fundamental ideas developed in Babylon, this type of astrology is also known as "judge" or "genetliac." This is the form of astrology that most of us know today if we are not believers or skeptics. The question of why people believe in astrology is more interesting than the details of the horoscope. Psychologists have shown that clients are satisfied with astrological predictions whenever procedures are individualized in a rather vague manner.

Astrology is best understood by learning how it started. Astrology is undoubtedly the oldest and, at the same time, currently the most popular of all pseudoscience. Astrology is also used to deepen the understanding of our nature. This psychological approach has increased significantly over the past 30 years, as more and more astrologers develop their counseling skills. Astrology is a magical thought, which gave us creationism and most forms of alternative medicine. It contradicts scientific reasoning and puts the practitioner exactly in opposition to the tradition of enlightenment.

Astrology is pseudoscience because people often believe in it for illegitimate reasons. He doesn't give examples here. Astrology is, in short, the study of the correlation between the astronomical positions of the planets and the events on Earth. Astrologers believe that the positions of the sun, moon and planets at the time of the birth of a person have a direct influence on the character of this person. Astrology is a wonderful blend of science, art and craftsmanship. The best part about this is that no matter how much you learn, you will never be able to embrace all your knowledge.

The belief in astrology is that the positions of certain celestial bodies affect or correlate with a personality trait of people. In the past, those who studied astrology used the observation of celestial objects and the creation of graphs of their movements. No prior knowledge of astrology is required. The four levels of study include all the astrological knowledge you need from the beginning to have your own successful practice. Astrology is called that because it comes from the stars, as it is called theology because it comes from God. To live astrologically is, with a pleasant concupiscence, to eat from the tree of knowledge of good and evil and to bring death to oneself.

A complete bibliography of astrology is beyond the scope of this frequently asked question, but some books have been included. Interested readers are invited to visit a well-stocked library. However, since the heavens were never intended for these purposes, astrology is a dangerous and illegal practice. Were the stars created to observe the calendar and declare God's Gloria? The lessons here are for everyone who wants to learn how to do Astrology. They are especially for skeptics because science requires that knowledge of a topic must pass before evaluation.

Because if astronomy is the study of the movements of celestial bodies, then astrology is the study of the effects of these movements. Astronomers of the ancient world assumed a division of the universe by which the higher and immutable bodies of the celestial worlds dominated the terrestrial or sublunar sphere, where everything was mortality and change. But astrology is no longer just love and money. Astrology Answers many other questions. Professional astrology is the art of helping others to help them find what they are called to do.

The practitioner of shamanic astrology is trained in the naked eye knowledge and experience of the night sky and the sacred rhythms, cycles, and movements of the cosmos. Astrology is also an art form, which lends itself to quick sketches and complex portraits of individuals, couples, businesses, Nations and more. Astrology can also clearly have spiritual and religious nuances, as evidenced by studies of ancient Egypt. Astrology is not scientific due to the fact of precession or displacement of constellations. Early astronomers were not aware of precession and therefore did not take it into account in their system.

While it is fun, the astrology of solar signs is a rather superficial and marginally useful application of a complex and ancient science that goes back thousands of years. Learn how astrology can be used to inform your decisions and increase your wisdom. Astrology is the ancient practice and study of stars and planets. Its history dates back to the Babylonian era. Astrology is a model.

Complete astrology is a way to interpret a horoscope so that all aspects are taken into account. We can observe trends in External areas such as professional, financial and social needs. That is why astrology is known as the "science of indications." Without an effort to overcome the impulse of a particular force or thrust of action, the indications suggest what it is likely to be, and in any case, astrology reveals the timing of trends and certain influences. Today, some astrology is presented in this way, but this is not true "traditional astrology." Did you know that astrology was considered a science in the ancient history of man?

Astrology is not a stupid old thing, superstition or pseudoscience, but a true science of human experience. Its symbols give way to the whims of human behavior, which can never be reduced to simple and absolute formulas. Perhaps there is hostility because astrology remains a living practice, a true competitor of popular respect and patronage. I hope that traditional hostility can die between historians and sociologists and a true understanding of this influential practice and belief. This does not mean that astrology is accurate to predict human behavior or events to a significantly greater degree than the simple case. There are many satisfied customers who believe that their horoscope accurately describes them and that their astrologer gave them good advice.

Astrology is harmless; it's entertainment. Whatever its past glory, it now looks like a five hundred vision of the cosmos. Astrology is perhaps the oldest and, even in a sense, the most ignored topic. It is the oldest because astrology was in existence in the distance we have been able to investigate the history of mankind. Instead, they like to provide anecdotal evidence-stories that people tell about how accurate they think astrology is. Anecdotal evidence is not acceptable in real science because it is too easy to omit all the negative experiences that people have, and people are not very good at accurately remembering and reporting experiences.

Astrology is based on birth cards for an individual. The position of the sun, moon and planets is traced in the zodiac at the time of birth. Also, astrology is not a quick study. Traditionalists used to say that it takes a student a transit Saturn, about 30 years old, to become an expert. Vedic astrology is part of a holistic and integrated knowledge system, and its effects can be enhanced by interacting with its "sister" sciences. The Vedic astrology system is kind because not only does a person tell you what could happen, but they are presented with a list of possible remedies or corrective measures to compensate for the amount and quality of karma coming back to them, as seen in the natal chart.

Astrology and the Renaissance

To put it simply, one would be tempted to say that this article on astrology in the Renaissance begins with Petrarch (1304-1374) and ends with Shakespeare (1564-1616). Petrarch, "the first man of the Renaissance," was not a fan of astrology and opposed to his fatalistic inclinations. "Free the ways of truth and life —these fireballs can't be guides for us. Illuminated by these rays, we do not need these deceptive astrologers and lying prophets who empty the coffers of gullible disciples of Gold, who deafen their ears with nonsense, try to corrupt with their mistakes, stop our present life, and afflict people with false fears of the futur. It is important to note from the beginning that the changes made in the Renaissance had a myriad of manifestations. As Richard Tarnas stressed in the passion of the spirit of the West," the phenomenon of rebirth lies in the great diversity of its expressions and in its unprecedented quality. The Renaissance is not expressed only through literature (or at the same time or place of the event) but through art, theology, the flourishing of science and discovery.

Reflecting on the Renaissance and its glories in art, music and literature and astrology, it is important to bear in mind that the notable changes of that era occurred in the context of plague, war, religious struggles, economic depression, the inquisition, and ecclesiastical conspiracies. In this vast expanse, we will try to determine the renewed interest and development of astrology during the Renaissance in this fascinating period of history.

Twin Stars: a change from Aristotle to Plato

The discovery and translation of ancient texts was an instigator of great transitions in history, particularly the works of Plato and Aristotle. In his book, sleepwalkers, Arthur Koestler commented on the influence and popularity of these Greek thinkers. "As for their influence in the future," writes Koestler, "Plato and Aristotle should be called Twin Stars with a single center of gravity, which surrounds and alternate projecting their light upon the generations that follow them. Each would have their turn to enjoy being "fashionable," while the other is out of fashion. According to Koestler, Plato would reign sovereign until the twelfth century, then Aristotle's work would be rediscovered, and after two centuries, when the world's thinkers tired of Aristotle's rhetoric, Plato would reappear in a different aspect. In the period up to the rise of the Renaissance, he was Aristotle's star to shine and, although it may be hard to believe, given the lack of approval of modern Christianity, to astrology, he was a school theologian, who united Aristotle, church doctrine and astrology.

Thomas Aquinas (1225-1274) seemed to have been in the right place at the right time with the right things to say. Arabic erudition and the possible translation of Aristotle's work into medieval Latin meant a rebirth for Aristotelian thought during Aquinas' lifetime. These works of Aristotle became an important project for this Dominican monk, a pupil of Albert Magnus (1206-1280), himself an Aristotelian translator. Tarnas noted that "Aquinas converted Aristotle to Christianity and baptized him. The emergence of Aristotelian thought in medieval times benefited astrology because of its view that "everything that happens in the sublunar world is caused and governed by the movements of the celestial spheres. Brahe's discoveries invalidated the notion of a separate "sublunar world. There was still the alignment of celestial bodies on Earth, and as a result, they have a greater influence on life on Earth. Astrology and alchemy used these same methods of Aristotelian logic but were not bound by the pedantry of the academic or completely subject to the dogma of the church: classical Astrology, often linked to medical studies and codified by Ptolemy, was taught in universities. Surely, you might have thought your influences would have been greater.

Astrologers, therefore, can predict the truth in most cases, especially when they make general predictions. In particular, predictions do not reach certainty because nothing prevents a man from resisting the diktats of his lower faculties. Therefore, astrologers themselves often say that "the sages rule the stars" because that is how they rule their own passions."

This avoids the dilemma that would bother humanists in the next century: the idea of free will.

Even with the support of Aquinas, this does not mean that the church supported all facets of astrology: there were quite clear boundaries. Medical astrology was acceptable while asking too deeply in the future might be considered walking on God's fingers. By the time, Aquinas had carefully reconciled Astrology / Astronomy and the church giving the condition of free will rather than absolute determinism.

At the dawn of the Renaissance, there is no doubt that astrology resurfaced despite being mocked almost simultaneously in three very different cultures. In addition to Petrarch's comments, the Muslim scholar Ibn Khaldun (1332-1406) condemned astrology as "all conjectures and conjectures based on astral influence (supposed to exist) and the resulting air conditioning. The Frenchman Nicholas Oresme, in 1370, wrote "many princes and magnates moved by a hurtful curiosity, try with vain arts to search for hidden things and investigate the future. For these men (including Petrarch), astrology has placed the overwhelming temptation before man to discover his future. Having established the existence of astrology before the Renaissance, the question of how it gained popularity despite being so deeply condemned remains.

One clue lies in a connection made between heaven and Earth in a more metaphorical sense. Aquinas had pointed out that there was a "principle of continuity" (as it will be called later) that connected higher beings with life forms increasingly lower than the kingdoms of Lucifer, elements of the orthodox doctrines of the Catholic Church. This was associated with a shift from another worldly asceticism to a positive view of life and, therefore, worthy of study. We can see this new vision reflected in Dante's Divine Commedia (1265-1321) with man at the center of an Aristotelian universe, balanced between heaven and Hell in a moral drama of Christianity. It should be noted that the universe of Aristotle, as well as that of Dante and Aquinas, was geocentric, a premise that, of course, would eventually be refuted. Dante's popular work shows how the "common" man of the time considered astronomy and theology to be inextricably linked, and, in a clear break in clerical tradition, it was written in a vernacular that even the most illiterate of the time could appreciate. Therefore, what was once only available to the higher classes or clergy had been made available to the general public.

Tarnas pointed out that if Dante's work culminated and summed up the medieval era, Petrarch expected and propelled a future era, bringing a revival of Culture, Creativity and human greatness. According to Tarnas, Petrarch was motivated by a new spirit but inspired by the ancients to create even greater glory with the man himself as the center of God's creation. Petrarch's ideal was erudite piety and called to memory the classical heritage of Europe through literature.

Even when the plague broke out, the idea that life should be appreciated rather than simply studied was evident in the work of Giovanni Boccaccio in The Decameron (1353). Boccace wrote about what life really was, rather than how the church thought it should be lived. The uncertainty of daily survival has created a general mood of morbidity, influencing people to "live for the moment." It would seem that even Petrarch was not immune to this new way of seeing life. In 1336, Petrarch climbed Mount Ventoux, which rises to more than six thousand feet, beyond the Vaucluse for the greatest pleasure of it. He read The Confessions of St. Augustine at the summit and reflected that his ascension was nothing more than an allegory of the aspiration for a better life. In his experience, perhaps we can understand why he was reluctant to accept being limited by destiny and refused to see himself "if it has no consequences in relation to God, the church, or nature."

During the years of the plague, when Europe turned its eyes to the authority of medicine at that time, the members of the College of Physicians of Paris delivered (in part) this reason for the Great Plague:

"From the astral influence that was considered the origin of the 'great mortality,' doctors and scientists were as fully convinced as they were of its reality. A great conjunction of the three higher planets, Saturn, Jupiter and Mars, in the sign of Aquarius, which took place, according to Guy de Chauliac, on March 24, 1345, was generally received as its main cause."

Petrarch was disappointed to realize that the plague he had claimed from so many people he loved was caused by large conjunction of planets in the air signals.

By the fifteenth century, Astrology had received an additional boost in the form of a Byzantine scholarship. In 1438, the Byzantine Emperor John VIII Palaeologus attended the Council of Ferrara and the Council of Florence to discuss a union of the Greek and Roman churches. With him was Plato's erudite plethon who generously offered to translate Plato's texts to interested Florentines. It was a fabulous improvement to the previous work on the translation of Petrarch and his contemporaries, as they were so hampered by their difficulties in translating Greek into Latin. Plethon (also known as George Gemistos) had "long nurtured an ambitious plan to restore the vitality of the pagan religion that belonged before Justinian's suppression of worship and the Athens Academy: in short, he was, in everything but the name, a "pagan" philosopher. As a total pagan, Plethon predicted that the world would forget Jesus and Cosimo de mici, head of the influential family bank Medici (who built his business empire in the economic depression after the bubonic plague) was so impressed by this "new" met opened an Academy platonic in 1439, and elected the promising young Marsilio Ficino (1433-1499) to manage it. Although, as a child, Ficino showed an early talent for translation and encouraged by the Medici family, he eventually translated a large number of ancient texts, including those of Plato and Hermes Trismegisto. Campion points out that Greek manuscripts also found their way west after the fall of Constantinople to the Turks in 1453. Because he had established himself as an interpreter, Many of these texts fell directly into Ficino's hands.

Ficino not only interpreted these texts but commented and was clearly influenced by them. His own contributions include three books on life ("De Triplici Vita"), which contains a book entitled on obtaining life from heaven ("De Vita Coelitus Comparanda"). Ficino was largely responsible for bringing back the Neoplatonic belief that the stars were divine. Reflections of this belief can be seen in the works of Michelangelo (1475-1564), Raphael (1483-1520), Da Vinci (1452-1519), Botticelli (1445-1510) and others. There was a general change in art during this period: previous artists had focused on recreating biblical images or symbols, while Renaissance artists began to study more closely the pattern of nature and to employ more realism in their work, adding more color and depth as Baigent so eloquently expressed Ficino's influence on these painters, a talisman capable of changing those who contemplated it. Frances Yates thus describes Botticelli's work and, in particular, his masterpiece, The Birth Of Venus, as a practical application of Ficino's magic by drawing "the venereal spirit of the star and transmitting it to the user or the viewer of its beautiful image.

Under this resurgence of neo-Platonism and a revival of pagan gods and goddesses, Astrology had also found favor through the use of almanacs and their popularity in various European courts. Without almanacs, astrology could have continued to be available only to those who could afford to read and write (i.e., royalty) had there not been one thing: The Invention of Johann Gutenberg's printing press in 1440. Until then, the printed material limited to the religious material copied on parchment, whose creation was taken as an act of worship (The Book OfKells, for example), was reproduced by hand and, therefore, quite rare. For example, an inventory of books from the University of Cambridge library, 1424, showed that the University owned only 122 books, each of which had a value equal to a farm or vineyard. The printing press allowed the reproduction of religious and secular texts. Astrological tables and almanacs were just one facet of the many themes that were suddenly made available to the new avid readers.

The tip of the attack

Thus, astrology, with its allusions to pagan gods and goddesses, reached the peak of its popularity. However, just as one would have thought astrology would be safe, an unprecedented posthumous attack came in 1494, delivered by a Ficino student, Pico della Mirandola. The peak attack has shaken astrology to the heart and is still cited as the most devastating attack of astrology in history. Cornelius characterized spike's attack as a "neo-Platonic interpretation of magic, using the weapons of Aristotelian logic," adding that at this time in our history, the imaginative consciousness called magic and the craft of horoscopic judgments were separated. After the peak, Horoscope craft never had a serious intellectual case.

There are some common misconceptions about this attack. This was certainly bad news for astrology in Italy. For example, in England, in the next century, Elizabeth I openly consulted the magician John Dee (1527-1608) for astrological advice. During Dee's stay in France, Jean-Baptiste

Morin (1583-1659) enjoyed, like Dee, a large number of followers in Europe. Secondly, the attack was not directed against astrology itself but against the abuse of practical astrologers. Campion points out that Pico's intention was more to reform astrology than to destroy it. Like any other Reformation, this astrological development will eventually focus on many astrological practices, such as erroneous astronomical tables and a geocentric universe, as well as developments outside the Ptolemaic system, such as new house systems.

It can not be denied that astrology's reputation had great success with Johann Stoeffler's prediction of a great flood during the great conjunction of the planets with Pisces in February 1524, a month known for its fine weather. Although the summer saw some notable rains, it was far from the great flood predictions that more than fifty astrologers had predicted following Stoeffler's predictions. However, this did little to eradicate Nostradamus's reputation (1503-1566), whose quartets were well known in his life.

The revolutionary idea of Nicolas Copernicus (1473-1543) of a universe centered on The Sun made little impression when, in the revolutions of the celestial spheres, it was published in 1543. Koestler says that not only was Copernicus a hard job to read, but he was also a worse seller. However, eventually, this work would transform man's view of the world from a Kosmos (in the Greek sense), where there was a proportionality between man and the universe, to the post-Renaissance heliocentric world associated with the development of modern science. Astrology requires this scale between man and the universe to thrive. With Galileo's best-seller in 1609, Siderius Nuncius, the heliocentric worldview, was catapulted into public consciousness.

About thirty-one years after Copernicus' death on November 11, 1572, Tycho Brahe, leaving an alchemical laboratory to pick up his dinner, noticed a new bright star near the constellation of Cassiopeus. About this event, says Koestler:

"The meaning of the sensational event was in the fact that it contradicted the basic doctrine, Aristotelian, Platonic and Christian—that all change, all generation and decay were confined in the immediate vicinity of the earth, the sphere sub-lunar; where, as the eighth distant sphere in which were placed the fixed stars was immutable from the day of creation."

Brahe's research had one feature difficult to find in Aristotelian logic: precision. The logic of time emphasizes quality rather than quantitative measurement; Brahe devotes himself to measurement, down to fractions of Arc minutes in his calculations, and does not tolerate the "close enough" attitude of planetary tables. Later, Brahe proved that the Great Comet of 1577 was not a sub-lunar object (the Aristotelian thought of time) but was "at least six times" in space as much as the moon. In the same year, Brahe, at his request, received the first watch with a minute hand from his inventor, Jost Burgi. Up to this point in history, the precise maintenance of time had been impossible.

A few years later, Astrology still suffered from the Papal Bull of 1585, which in fact, prohibited judicial astrology and dictated the closure of all serious astrological publications except for the simplest of pamphlets (the same things Pico disputed). As a fairly traditional, if not conservative, discipline, astrology has not been helped by a major paradigm shift in cosmology. When a cold and hungry Johannes Kepler (1571-1630) appeared at the gate of Brahe in 1600, it was only a matter of time that the world was convinced that the earth revolved around the sun.

If the "scientific" side of astrology began to unravel, it hardly influenced the affection of the Elizabethan audience for this. William Shakespeare makes more than a hundred allusions to astrology in his thirty-seven plays. In its time, planets and stars were personified, heavenly spheres had eternal souls, and people were afraid to change the traditional order of things. "The heavens themselves, the planets and this center observe degree, priority and place, but when the planets in bad mixtures of disorder wander, what pests and what presence! Another example of this can be seen in the storm of Shakespeare, such as The magician of the success (a character loosely based on the astrologer of Queen Elizabeth, John Dee), is portrayed as the cause of a great storm and subsequent sinking, with the great dismay of his young daughter, Miranda. It seems such an ironic but kind tribute to astrology that this work's characters were used to name the satellites of the planet Uranus when they were discovered in the middle of the XIX century. It could almost look like an olive branch, from astronomy to astrology.

Helpful Advice On How To Learn Astrology

The best way to learn astrology is to study the current astrological locations of planets and understand the correlation between symbolic representations of planetary models and political, environmental and social events in the world.

Astrology tip number one: follow current events.

By following current astrological movements and changes, you will get an idea of the different positions of the planets and understand the different ways in which these configurations manifest themselves. For example, today,s there is a powerful configuration that represents revolutionary and disgusting ideas. When the planets aligned and moved to these positions, the protest in the Middle East began. When you study astrology by following the current positions of the planets, you will not only be able to predict or understand world events, but you will also be able to interpret how these planetary models play on personal astrological maps.

Astrology tip number two: Understand and track transits to your astrology card.

In addition to tracking the current astrological movements of the planets, it is very important to track the astrological energies in relation to your personal chart. When a planet in a current position in the sky makes a mathematical corner for a planet's Natal position on the astrology chart, then your personal planet is under an astrology transit. For example, if you were born with your Sun in Aries and Uranus in Aries is in the same degree as your Sun, then you are under Uranus's transit to your Sun. Especially Uranus joins your Sun. This would indicate a moment in your life for your personal "revolution" of change.

Astrology Tip Number Three: find a good Astrology course or astrology workshop.

There are many ways to study astrology, but it can be very complex and confusing if you don't have a system that allows you to learn Astrology easily and effortlessly. Although, as with any new teaching acquiring knowledge requires a little effort, but the best way is to learn from an experienced astrologer who makes complicated concepts understandable. Find an astrology course that is designed around the current principles of astrology and how astrological influences affect the astrology chart. Find an astrologer you love and an astrology teacher who has experience. Of course, you can learn from someone you don't like, but why? It is better not to have a personality barrier between you and the subject you are learning.

Astrology tip number four:

Write your life story. Probably the best way to learn astrology is to create an autobiography of the events that occurred in your life. Take your time to really remember important moments and all the memories you can. Like the first time you fell in love, your graduation, your first job, any major job changes, getting married, having children, getting divorced, big or tragic love stories, moving, traveling. Enter the dates of these events. So you're going to do a survey Astrology job to determine what transits or planetary influences were occurring at that time.

Astrology Council number five: go to astrology conferences.

There is nothing like going to astrology conferences to get a taste of the complexity and diversity that astrology offers. Look for regional and national conferences offered around the country, or if you have a strong Jupiter, Research Astrology conferences around the world, why not? It is fun to study astrology with like-minded astrologers who meet at Astrology conferences. In addition to astrology lessons, many conferences offer astrology workshops before and after the conference.

Astrology is a fascinating discipline and can be overwhelming when you start learning Astrology. Don't let complexity frustrate you by learning this beautiful gift of the universe that can help you understand yourself and the world around you. Learn to be a co-creator with the powerful forces of the planets. Learn Astrology, be your astrologer and master this secret and ancient discipline of esoteric knowledge and intuition

Vedic Astrology Helps Steer Key Life Decisions

We all have concerns about our future, life, family, wealth and health. Many of us respond to our personal and professional concerns using the influence of astrology. While astrology is a fairly extensive field with many branches and religions, Vedic astrology is considered a strong belief system that originated in India centuries ago. Today, Vedic astrology constitutes an important belief system and orientation method for many people, both in India and in countries like the United States, United Kingdom, Canada, Australia, etc.

In general, it is believed that most of the misfortunes, setbacks, losses, illnesses and delays are caused by planetary movements or "yoga," which are in unfavorable positions. Different planetary positions cause astrological situations, namely, KaalSarp Dosh, Manglik Dosh, Pitra Dosh, Sade Sati. It is said that many of these astrological positions are responsible for causing alterations in marriage, life, romance, careers and education.

Since astrology is not an exact science and knowledge of specialized astrological interpretations is not common, there have been cases when the facts have been misinterpreted. Precise interpretation and intervention in Vedic astrology require special experience and practice.

Vedic astrology, as a discipline, addresses all aspects of human life: spiritual, physical, mental and emotional. The basis of Vedic astrology is based on planetary movements and positions with respect to time and its impact on living beings on Earth. In Vedic astrology, there are 27 constellations, including the 12 signs of the zodiac, 9 planets and 12 houses, each house and planet symbolizes one aspect of human life, and a person, time, place of birth indicates how the 12 signs are distributed between the 12 houses and 9 planets. The map, which represents signs and planets, is widely known as a horoscope chart.

For centuries, Vedic astrology has been used as an exceptional system of prediction and calculations. These calculations are based on the positions of stars and planets and are in phase for each zodiac sign under which individuals can be born. Vedic astrology allows people to identify what could happen in their future lives and advises possible remedies to help the situation. The idea behind the conviction is to identify incoming threats and avoid them before they occur. The Hindu astrologer uses appropriate and accurate tools to detect clues in an individual's life that could help them avoid certain accidents that occur. Astrologers often use birth cards to predict the Bhavishya (future) of an entity. The Vedic astrologer says that Indian Vedic astrology also follows the Dasha system, which is based on the Native Moon in the natal chart. It is also considered an accurate indicator of future events.

Understanding the relationship between planets, stars and chakras, astrologers perceive where energy flows or matter does not flow. This can be related to all forms of healing, whether emotional, sexual, physical, karmic, mental or energetic. In these technologically advanced times, we can find many resources and tools to determine our Bhavishya. The internet has given us the opportunity to contact live astrologers and discover what lies on our way, all from the comfort of our home. Vedic astrology can help us see our true principle of soul level in life.

Rebecca Hood

Tarot

For Beginners

A Complete Guide to Discover the Secrets of Tarot Reading

What is Tarot?

The Tarot (also known as Tarock, Tarokk, Tarot, and similar names) is a family of trick-taking card games. The game has expanded to 78 cards, which contain legal documents for each of the four semi-regular dress, to win a permanent 21 cards, and a kind of "wild card" with the name "mad" or "I'm sorry." Even Though it is regarded primarily by many as a means of predicting the future or divination, the Tarot deck was created in Northern Italy during the 15th century as play cards. The idea of winning a suit that survives in such popular card games as spades and Hearts comes from the Tarot game.

The myth of the Egyptian origin of tarot cards, although once common, has long been revealed by later scholars, before the eighteenth. For centuries, there is no trace of tarot cards used for occultism or prophecy. Popular tarot readings at Renaissance fairs are a creative license taken with a historical fact and should not be considered authentic. Contrary to popular belief, classic playing cards were not derived from Tarot card games, and the Fool is not related to The Joker of classic playing cards. The Joker was created in the United States during the 19th century originally for the card game Euchre.

There are two types of Tarot deck.

The appropriate Italian Tarot

The traditional game of Italian, suitable for coins, cups, swords, and batons, is currently favored by those who use Tarot cards, divination. However, in some countries such as Italy and Switzerland, these decks are still used for the game. Those who practice tarot prophecy often call coins "pentagons" and "wands." With a few exceptions, trump the Italian Tarot adapted the scene varies little from one platform to another and are often regarded by Tarot readers as containing a symbolic meaning. The depiction of Papessa (II) and the pope (in) on related Italian Tarot Cards has been controversial in some regions. In Switzerland, these images were replaced by images of Juno (II) and Jupiter (V.). In Bologna, the papal figurines with Empress (III) and Emperor (IV) were replaced by four figures of moresche, which are not numbered and serve as triumphs of the same status in the Bologna Tarot variety. The system of Italian or Spanish costumes is not limited to tarot cards. This suit system is a common regional model of classic playing cards in southern Europe and Latin America.

French tarot

Tip card with a French or international outfit, tiles, heart, spades, Clover is now used in countries such as France and Austria for the game. In France and southern Germany, Roman numerals have been abandoned in favor of Arabic numerals, while in some countries, such as Austria, Roman numerals are still used. Trump Images appropriate to the French Tarot often depict scenes of people at work and play, and real and mythological animals and landscapes, the regional space. In some regions such as Austria and southern Germany, the game is reduced to 54 cards with the removal of the lower pip card. Unlike the relevant Italian decks, there is a wide variety of images on French tarot cards. On the decks of the French Tarot, a mad man is often depicted as a musician, harlequin, or other types of artist. French Tarot Cards are rarely used for divination.

Common rules of the game

At each turn, players must follow, if possible. If the seeds are not possible, it will be necessary to reproduce the resource. If the players are empty in the suit played and are also empty in the cards, then any card can be played. The winner of one round leads another.

There is a noticeable variation in how a fool or an excuse is used. In countries like France and Italy, The Fool is a "wild card" that can be played in any order, to avoid having to follow suit, while in some countries like Austria and South Germany, the Fool is simply the biggest asset.

Many modern tarot games include offers to determine who will become the recipient and play alone against other players. In some tarot cards with four or more players, the recipient of the card called the king or the high-ranking card chooses a partner, whose identity remains secret until the called card is played.

The values of Cards where "n" is often equal to 1, 2, 3 or 4 depending on the type of game played, are presented as follows:

Trump XXI (21), Trump I (1), the excuse or the fool, and the four Kings are worth $4 + 1/n$ each

The four queens are worth $3 + 1/n$ each

The four Knights or Knights are worth $2 + 1/n$ each

The four sockets are worth $1 + 1/n$ each

All other cards have a value of $1/n$ each

The usual goal of Tarot card games is to score more card points, as well as any other bonus point, which may also be available depending on the regional variant you are playing.

Tarot reading and divination

Although they were originally designed for card games, Tarot Cards are generally regarded by many as a splitting tool, especially in regions where Tarot card games remain largely unknown. There are many published bridges that are dedicated today for the purpose of divination. The most famous bridge designed for divination or "getting information" is the Tarot Rider Waite Smith.

Using fortune-telling cards, they are arranged in a pattern. These patterns, usually in the form of a cross, are known as "throws" or "spreads." "Queerer," which is the one who aspires to read the tarot cards, mixes the package and asks the question in the cards. The question could be "yes" or "no" of a more general type or nature. The reader organizes the cards into the proliferation of choice and allegedly tries to answer the question using the cards as a guide. The divinatory interpretation of a Tarot card often depends on the vertical or inverted direction of the card or its juxtaposition with other cards. Sometimes only 22 cards from the Tarot deck are used. These cards, called "Major Arcane" by Tarot readers, include 21 triumphs and one Fool. The remaining 56 cards are called "minor arcane."

Not all Tarot readers call themselves "fortune tellers" when they claim not to use cards for predictive purposes. In recent years, "psychological" rather than paranormal interpretations have been guided by a context in which a lot of tarot data is visible. These tarot data are called "introspective" in nature and do not make supernatural or prophetic statements. Tarot reading has recently become popular in some circles as a reflection tool in an attempt to increase your creativity. It should be noted, however, that there is no empirical evidence of psychic phenomena or therapeutic benefits of Tarot data.

Different Types of Tarot Packs

Initially, tarot cards were the type of game in Italy. However, people adopted them in the psychic reading and turned out to be accurate. Today, it remains one of the most popular psychic tools in the West, and many people believe in the value of this gain. There are many types of tarot cards, and some of them include:

Ator: it has a refreshing new look that makes it suitable for the next generation psychic readings. He uses adorable characters, which is the reason for his popularity among many people.

Benedetti is on a richly painted gold leaf. This is the ideal choice for readers who want to add a touch of class and character to their service. Visconti's maps inspired them.

Cat people tarot: for those who want to glimpse the Earth that is far away, Cat People tarot is a perfect choice. Expresses human imagination with mystics and cats.

Some psychological readers have adopted the psychedelic chromatic approach to their psychological data. For them, the Smith Tarot column is a perfect choice. The most unusual and least used modern tarot is a curious tarot. It is distinguished by strange characters that attract the attention of many people. This is a rare type of Tarot card because readers are afraid that it will frighten customers.

The Golden Tarot: for great thinkers, it is available. Many readers have used gold tarot cards in the past.

International tarot icon: for a more fun approach to tarot data, an international Tarot icon from Switzerland is available. This is their version of traditional tarot data.

Love craft tarot: for fans of Ancient Writings, this tarot is a tribute to one of the ancient writers.

Tarot de Marseille: for the best divination for ordinary people, Tarot de Marseille is easily available and accessible in many stores around the world. It was also common for people to use tarot cards for meditation purposes.

Thin: thin Tarot contains about 97 tarot cards more than any other set of tarot cards. Many consider it one of the most powerful oracle cards. For New Tarot students, the Palladini Tarot deck is best suited. Connect the future with the old Tarot data. It represents elements of ancient Egyptian Art, so it prefers art lovers.

For a new generation of Tarot readers, Phoenix Tarot Cards are more suitable. This is a product of the 20th century. It includes bright colors, and therefore very pleasing to the eye.

Many people go for tarot data to predict the events of his future and the luck or tragedy that may happen. Fear of the unknown is a determining factor for Tarot business data. Depending on their preferences, tarot readers can choose one of the above tarot cards for their business.

How Does Tarot Reading Work?

People often ask how tarot cards, which are collected by the game in random order, can significantly affect the lives of people. It is generally excluded that the tarot cards may not communicate the action you need in a given situation, but rather to give you options, or different directions that you can take. There are many theories about how tarot cards can be so effective. We will examine two of the main theories behind tarot cards in this article.

The first of these theories about the functioning of tarot reading is synchronicity. It is believed that the universe will lead us in the right direction by accident. Basically, these are signs that say, "Hey, do this" or "you should try it." The use of quantum mechanics can partially explain synchronicity and tarot cards. Without going into a full-blown discussion on quantum mechanics, it is safe to say that there are forces in quantum mechanics that have a very real effect on physical objects. It is believed that these energies affect the cards that read tarot cards.

Another Tarot theory is projection. Some believe that we project our beliefs and thoughts about reading tarot and get the result we expect. In other words, you'll find what you're looking for. If this theory of Tarot is true, then the tarot can become a very useful tool. I mean that it will help you connect with your true desires, emotions, and feelings, which are grown in your subconscious mind. Tarot reading, when it comes to research in our subconscious, may be related to the ink point test that we all know. I should say that Tarot Cards are more support to find out what's inside, and a way to talk to your Higher Self.

To perform a tarot reading, you don't need the funds, but some believe that means it is better for the energy they provide. There are two different types of tarot data. The first is the question of the Tarot. It is there that tarot reading is used to answer a particular question. As a rule, you are looking for an answer, "yes or no." Try to look at this kind of tarot reading as a guide to help you make a decision. When you ask a question, try to ask in a general overview, with some details, but not too detailed. When you ask a question in tarot, it is also better to focus the question on you. I am referring to questions about what can be done to change, improve, or change the situation. It is also better to ask the question in a neutral way. Try not to ask the question from a narrow point of view. This will give you a wider range of possible answers and solutions. Of course, when doing a tarot, you want to stay positive in your questions and expectations.

Another type of Tarot is the so-called open reading. This kind of tarot reading is designed to give you a complete overview of your life. When doing this type of tarot reading, you can be a little specific and get information on such areas as Love, Money, Health, and relationships.

When the tarot is made, usually, the person who receives the reading shuffles the cards. It's time to stay in the moment and focus on what you want to discover by reading tarot cards. After the game has been mixed, the person who makes the Tarot Reading will put the cards in a scatter. In a tarot reading, the placement of cards in the span makes sense with the card itself. Different Tarot Cards are used depending on the nature of your question, the reader, and the allotted time.

Surprisingly, tarot cards can be extremely accurate. I strongly recommend people to try to experiment with reading tarot. I think you may be surprised by the answers that come to mind, as well as the problems that are solved.

How Self Development with the Tarot works

You can think about why you want to read tarot cards, and you can focus on the things that help tarot cards reading, what you have in mind. Try asking a question before you see the tarot reader. Do not think that Tarot Cards are designed to match yes or no. If you see the leadership in the Tarot from the reader, you can also feel better at the end of the session. Also, ask reasonable questions. You can also have a clearer view of how to see further into the future.

Some may feel as if Tarot has helped to overcome the situation, which could stand in the presence of life and may eventually see a change. Numbers can be useful in some decisions in your life. They can lead you. Some people need guidance only for a short time when collecting ideas. There are many interpretations of some tarot cards.

Even if you are a beginner, you can still read tarot cards. The best resources you can find on the internet regarding the type of Tarot that you want to use, whether it be online, face to face, or by email, CD or tape, or even books. There are also various articles available for reading in all of the above items that you can refer to. The sites are available for anyone to check out the different and variable Tarot Cards. Tarot cards for centuries claim that they offer or even help to answer all the provocative questions in life.

Tarot cards have advantages and limitations. Everyone decides no matter where he is in his life. Tarot does not work miracles and does not replace any medical care and other medications. Tarot cannot physically help you with any problem that you may have; they can only guide you. They cannot answer whether you will marry or have a child on a given day or date.

There are different sets of cards, depending on the type of Tarot card or packages that you can read. If you are interested in reading tarot cards, you can always search the internet for more questions that you can lay on the cards. Tarot cards can be very accurate in terms of events or what happened to this person. The Internet is the fastest way to find out more information about tarot cards.

Tarot data is available to people if they need to contact them and compare them by images or numbers on tarot cards. People can be emailed Tarot Cards. It is entirely up to the individual if they want to know by different methods. There's an encyclopedia on tarot cards.

You can also do a personal journal once the Tarot is being taught, and maybe a reflection of what a person did in this life is the way of life.

There are also courses that can be taught on tarot cards. There are many websites that can be checked; also, many pictures of tarot cards can be seen on them as well.

There are many decks or tarot cards that can vary around the world; it serves many purposes in your life and journey. Tarot has a confusing history. Cards can always be studied on the course, if possible. The results of tarot cards can be achieved by analyzing the card. Tarot cards can be a good thing when you focus on what you're thinking right now. Good luck reading the Tarot. Bring more tarot messages.

What is Paranormal Tarot Cards Reading?

The history of paranormal Tarot Cards is something that is disguised by time. There are some testimonials and scientists who combine the source of the Tarot with that of ancient Egypt. At the same time, other teachers and the researchers suggest that the spelling of the sources of happiness with a very ancient bohemian refinement. However, more scientists add an Italian source to the tarot cards, and it is believed that Tarot cards have become psychic tools near 1400. From this experience, many different types have evolved and are only used now. One of the popular Bridges is the Rider-Waite Bridge.

A typical tarot deck contains 78 cards consisting of the four seeds seen in normal card games, which are hearts, diamonds, shovels, and clubs. The Latin version of the tarot game has a different set of outfits. These are swords, batons, mugs, and coins. Like a normal game, the tarot cards are numbered from one to ten plus four court cards, jack, queen, king, and Ace.

The difference between the tarot deck and the regular deck is 21 divine cards known as major Arcans. The equivalent tease in the game Tarot is called a fool, or an excuse. A fool can take all four seeds and act as the strongest good.

Reading a tarot card is easy because each trump card has a separate meaning. However, if you want to read the meaning of collecting cards, you need to make an interpretation. These maps have astrological links to data located in the context of the Octavian calendar. It is believed that tarot cards easily describe the physical and emotional characteristics of the subject.

The rich and centuries-old tradition of tarot reading is constantly evolving over time. Methods of interpretation of tarot cards continue to develop to achieve the culture in which they live. Changing the meaning can also contribute to the development of the Charter itself. Elements of the Tarot Card today are very different from what they were before.

Many tarot data are done face to face. You can find someone who reads tarot cards in your area by doing an online search, check local ads, or asking in an occult library. You should come prepared with a question or query much of the time, and you may find that if you can get useful ideas from the reading, it is more of a perceptive tool than a truly esoteric tool. Each Tarot reader has his own preferences on how to arrange cards and read them; however, one can reasonably expect that more complex and longer reading will be more expensive.

You can also have tarot reading on your phone. If you cannot find a local person who makes tarot reading or prefer extra discretion, it may be a good choice. Although you should expect that reading tarot on your phone will be quite expensive, avoid questionable minute-by-minute billing services. There are reliable Tarot readers who provide data over the phone at a reasonable flat rate. Some may also offer online readings for a small amount, and provide their interpretation of the maps through email.

Tarot cards have existed for centuries and have been used in many cultures for divination purposes. There are different card layouts, and there are different card reading methods that card readers use. The interpretation of Tarot Cards is based on the position of the card and the different symbols of each card.

Amateur Tarot Card Readings

As a beginner Tarot student, your choice of Tarot card games is the key to a successful understanding of the messages that the cards offer. It is important to find a tarot package that fits your style and personality and makes you comfortable. Some decks like Minchiate Tarot have additional cards that are not best for beginners but are an exception. As a Tarot novice, you will always have to choose in terms of beautiful Tarot game full of symbolism, so the problem is less to find a great set of tarot cards and more choose only one.

Eclectic Tarot

This page is probably the most comprehensive directory of tarot decks available for free online. While some of the more modern decks might not be there, it's a great place to shop for Windows Tarot deck suitable for beginners. This site also has a lot of tips and tutorials on the Tarot and its history, and it is a great free resource for your Tarot related questions. With over 1200 tarot and Oracle decks reviewed, and more added every day, you'll have plenty of starter tarot packages to choose from.

Llewellyn Worldwide

Llewellyn is an international new age publisher and has a huge collection of tarot games, books, and individual decks with beautiful artwork. You can browse some of the cards in many decks, and even get a free Tarot reading using a selection of them, which can be great if you try to figure out whether you connect with the specific symbolism of a deck or not.

Beetle

Scarabeo is an Italian publisher of tarot cards and books, among other topics related to divination, and their modern website offers a look at their extensive collection of tarot cards. They have a whole collection dedicated to tarot sets, which include introductory books with the bridge. If you are in the Gothic style artwork, they have several modern bridges inspired by fantastic creatures, such as fairies, mermaids, and vampires.

Choosing A Tarot Game For Beginners

There are no strict rules on that Tarot Cards are better to know about tarot cards, but many people will recommend easier decks near to the original tarot decks, than more modern with non-traditional card names or extra cards. However, it is important to choose a package that suits your personality, and many tarot readers will buy only those packages that I personally find beautiful or somehow attract. Navigate until you find a bridge that forces you to buy and use it to take your first steps into the Tarot world.

Tarot Through the Ages

Tarot, pictures, we are more familiar with today, evolved from the genre, board games, played in the 15th century in Italy, and it became popular throughout Europe over the next four centuries.

To thoroughly explore the history of Tarot, you can read Michael Dummet's great book, " The Game of Tarot: From Ferrara to Salt Lake City "(Duckworth, 1980). Dummet, a highly esteemed British philosopher, is the author of many books on tarot cards. His Tarot scholarship is extensive and provides much of the research available at the beginning of the Tarot deck and its variations.

Tarot originally was fun in the classroom for leisure, those with time and money to spend on games. I am sure that at that time, the cards were handmade and illustrated by artists, and each set would vary with the artist's individual representation of the card images. Especially from the 15th up to the 18th century in Europe, variations of tarot games were very popular and enjoyed by people of little wealth and intellect, very similar to chess or bridge. The Tarot of 1700 was a total madness throughout the continent.

There are several decks of tarot cards that have come to represent a familiar iconography, each with its own history, interpretation, and devotees. 15th-century Italian bridge Visconti-Sforza is probably the oldest surviving bridge of this era, with original cards in the collections of several museums around the world. These beautiful artistic images are often reproduced.

And the 19th-century version from the south of France, known as the Tarot of Marseille, is a very popular deck in Europe.

In the US, The Rider-Waite-Smith Tarot deck is most often used today. It was conceived by the well-known Tarot authority A. email. Waite, and published in 1902 by Ryder Co., the simplified graphic style of this deck retains the historical symbolism of previous decks, but seems to be fresh and accessible to modern sensibilities.

Other tarot scholars are convinced that Tarot has its roots even earlier. They see relationships with the Kabbalah, or with ancient Egyptian hieroglyphs. Cards, for games or prophecies, were used in China centuries before they found their way to Europe in the 14th century, and it can be the original embodiment of the Tarot.

It is more likely that Tarot cards were brought to Europe through card games that were popular in the Old World Of Arabia. In France in the 18th Century, Antoine Court De Gebelin promoted the concept that Tarot cards came from mystical practices in ancient Egypt, which is described in his multi-volume work, Le Monde Primitif. Another Frenchman, Etteillla, is considered the first to recreate the tarot as a "divination" device. Basically, it is the first tarot reader. Reproductions of his book Thoth Tarot and other publications of Etteilla are still available today.

Tarot Reading turned out to be a new construction during the embrace of the Victorian age of spiritualism and occultism, laying the foundation for what would become the Tarot of the New Age School we know today.

There is an extensive scholarship and research on the history of tarot cards, either from online sources or in libraries, for those interested in exploring the topic. But for most of us, the story is not as convincing as the question of how Tarot makes sense in our lives.

Steps To Giving a Great Tarot Reading

Becoming a good Tarot reader requires much more than remembering the meaning of tarot cards and knowing tarot cards. Reading tarot requires practice, patience, and, most importantly, the willingness to trust your own intuition. If you are reading for yourself or someone else, there are some very useful procedures to ensure good reading.

1. Prepare a quiet environment

Believe it or not, the environment in which you run and read tarot cards can significantly affect the reading. Not only can the environment affect you as a tarot reader, but it can also have consequences for the person being read. When reading tarot cards, it is always important to postpone your personal problems and fears. Creating a comfortable space to help you stay focused and calm will help you stay objective and neutral while reading. Rituals like lighting candles or burning incense can also help you get in the mood.

2. Choose a meaningful map

When reading tarot cards, significant cards serve as a representation of the person being read or the situation asking. If you use the card-marking to represent the reading in person, most of the readers of Tarot cards tend to use the court cards either by associating the physical attributes of the researcher with one of the court cards or by a combination of their astrological sign to one of the court cards. If you choose and the Access Map has a specific situation, you can be creative as you like. Depending on the severity of the application, you can choose a map of the main arcane or smaller arcane. Major arcane cards tend to be used for major environmental issues, while less obscure cards tend to focus on everyday concerns.

Meaningful maps will also help you stay focused on the person you are reading. In many tarot cards, this means that the cards are located in the center. Help the tarot reader interpret and help him identify the key questions that lie around the interviewer.

3. Choosing the right course of Tarot

Tarot decks are the layout of cards arranged in a certain scheme. Each location of the map in the range has a specific meaning. When individual Tarot Cards are assembled for the spread of tarot cards, their meanings can be used to create a kind of story. The Tarot reader then interprets the cards according to their position and the relationships between them at the bow.

As a tarot reader, it is important to choose the spread of Tarot, which corresponds to the question asked. If the question is, for example, about love, then you probably want to enjoy the spread of love. In some cases, it is recommended to create your own spread of tarot cards. This can be especially useful when it comes to more than one topic.

4. Formulation of questions

The way the interviewer frames or asks a question before reading it can have a significant effect on the overall usefulness of reading. The more accurate the interviewer with his question, the more likely it is that reading tarot cards will solve their problem in a particular way. It is also useful to put an end to this question. Open questions can reveal hidden or overlooked questions that would otherwise have been overlooked. Open questions can also help the tarot reader discover the main problems or other influences that can affect the person reading them.

5. Mixing Boards

There are several approaches to mixing cards before tarot reading. This is usually the point where you have to actually read touch the card (although some tarot readers don't want anyone to manipulate their cards). If you decide to leave the investigator to manipulate the cards, you need to make sure that they are responsible, focusing on how to mix so that this energy can be transferred to the card. There are also several approaches to the "cutting" of paper, among the most popular are that the interviewer cuts the bridge three times with his left hand.

6. How do I know your tarot pack?

Before giving tarot reading, I always encourage people to give them time to really know the Tarot game that will work. This will help you not only to get acquainted with the cards, but also to deepen the understanding of their importance and mutual interconnection in the spread of tarot. Inevitably, those who receive and read tarot cards as they will, always take your relationship with their own cards. If you do not know the game with which you work, it is likely to come when reading tarot cards.

Things You Didn't Want to Know About Tarot

Do you love tarot cards because of its aura of mystery, esoteric history, or magical qualities? If you think that Tarot Cards are peculiar because of one of these reasons, you will not like what I have to say in this book.

I will look at the real history of Tarot, and my research on it has led me to conclusions that are different from what most of you have read online, and may be different from the one that wants you to believe are the facts behind Tarot.

I enjoy using tarot cards for over 25 years, and I love tarot symbology and tarot divination. Still, I don't like it when uninformed people create a romantic/mystical fantasy story for these cards.

I collected the first ten pieces of information that I think tarot readers need to know about the origins of Tarot. These data were collected by art historians, map collectors, and my research in museums and libraries.

Number 1

For those of you who like the idea that Tarot Cards are a magical or mystical instrument that has been handed down since the Egyptian or even the Atlantis era, I'm sorry, but there is absolutely no evidence of that. Not only is there no evidence, but when you look at the first known tarot cards and look at how they were born, there is not even a possibility of connection with Egypt or the mythical Atlantis. I hear you say, "But I've seen maps that have Egyptian drawings or symbols on them!" And you might have, but these are subsequent additions to the work of Tarot, and the images on which the Tarot is based on do not have Egyptian drawings or symbols.

The First Surviving Tarot Cards are hand-painted decks that were made in Italy, around the year 1441. They were made for the Court of Filippo Maria Visconti, Duke of Milan (from 1412 to 1447), and these cards are known as Visconti-Sforza Tarot. This name was given to them because it was the name of the families for which these cards were created. We know this because the heraldry of these families was included in the maps themselves. Representations of family members are also used in Maps.

Number 2

It has been claimed that today's ordinary playing cards are derived from tarot cards. The Joker is a representative of the card of the Madman of the major Arcans. Sorry, but ordinary playing cards developed much earlier and entered Europe from the Islamic world around 1375.

Number 3

The combinations of tarot cards, as we know them, are very different from the original ones. Tarot costumes derive from Islamic playing cards that were coins, cups, swords, and Polo sticks. The game of polo was very important in Islamic culture, but it was not known in Europe when the cards arrived, so the suit of Polo sticks became known as the suit of sticks or sticks. In Italy and Spain, playing cards preserved the costumes of batons, coins, cups, and swords.

Number 4

Tarot costumes, as we know them, have evolved from these Islamic playing cards, and various occultists over the years have changed the original costumes to make the Tarot more magical or mysterious. Sticks/sticks/slats were changed to chopsticks, and the costume of coins was changed to Pentacles.

Number 5

For many years, there was a theory that gypsies brought tarot cards to Europe, and this notion, unfortunately, became an accepted "fact" in the history of tarot cards. However, we know that the Gypsies arrived in Western Europe in 1417, but playing cards were known in Catalonia, a region of northeastern Spain, in 1370, so the cards arrived 47 years earlier than the Gypsies. And in historical documents, gypsies are called only palm readers; they are not talked about using cards for divination until 1891. And even then, the cards they refer to are standard playing cards, not Tarot Cards.

Number 6

Tarot cards were not intended as a means of hiding esoteric information from ignorant or invasive Nations. There are many references to tarot during the 15th century, and all refer to tarot as a game. It is never mentioned as having been used in any other form during this period. It was conceived as a game and no esoteric connection, nor divinatory properties, was attributed to it until several centuries later. The most likely reason for his invention was that the Duke of Milan (Filippo Maria Visconti) wanted a variation on the standard playing card set he had used. He asked his artist Bonifacio Bembo to create an extension of this game.

Number 7

The images of cards in modern Tarot Cards are similar in some respects to the original tarot cards created by Bembo, but there have been some changes. Over the years, images on maps have been modified by occultists to make them more magical or mysterious. A good example of these changes is the card known as the fool. Rather than being shown as a naive and confident soul who dragged through the countryside with his faithful dog, he was originally depicted in rags, looking quite miserable. He was considered the weakest of all in the physical field. It was the classic "village idiot." The charter called the High Priestess was known as the Popess. The heiress was once called the Pope. The Hermit was known as the hunchback or the father. The Hanged Man was the traitor, and the judgment was known as the Angel.

Number 8

The main Arcane maps are based on Christian principles, not on esoteric or magical knowledge. For the major Arcanes, the artist, Bembo, decided to use an allegory of religious teachings that could easily be displayed in a series of images. If you look at the sources of the XV and XVI centuries and some of the first bridges that list the elements in a sequence, you will see a separate model emerge. This model shows the physical kingdom as the lowest form of existence, and then shows the path of Christian spirituality leading to their God. The last map of the Greater Arcane is the map of the world, and one of the first authors on the subject described this last map, as "the world," which is God the father. The terms "major arcane" and "minor arcane" are relatively recent terminology. Paul Christian, an occultist of the 1800s, introduced these terms in the Tarot. Again, these terms were given to tarot cards to make it more magical and mysterious. The word Arcana means mysterious or secret, and by granting the cards these Latin titles, it was imbued with a mystical quality that was never wanted by the original designers of the game.

Number 9

Some occultists believe that there is a direct link between the 22 ways of the Cabal and the major Arcanes. Pico della Mirandola was responsible for introducing the Cabal to Western occultists. Still, he did so more than 40 years after the existence of the Tarot cards, so the tarot images were certainly not based on or related to this Hebrew alphabet and magic system. If the cabalists had invented tarot cards, the first cards had Hebrew letters on them; and they would not have used images such as death or the devil, or photos of women on them. Jewish Kabbalists did not like images of this nature, nor those of the human form, because they were forbidden by the first commandment which constituted "cut images." And on the contrary, tarot cards do not appear in any way in kabbalistic literature. Tarot cards do not descend from Jewish culture, and Jewish cabalists today do not recognize tarot cards as part of their beliefs.

Any meaning between the Tarot and the Cabal is the result of four main things;

1) the occultists conveniently hid some basic ideas about the Cabal to better fit their theory about a game between the two subjects. For example, papers such as the Pope and The Last Judgment are obviously Christian, not Jewish.

2) when designing a Tarot deck, occultists often implanted additional symbols inside the Tarot card images to satisfy the Cabal. For example, Levi introduced on the magician's table the signs of the "elementary" suit to prove that this card represented "First matter" - the elements are the basis from which all things were composed.

3) occultists often organized the order of cards to better fit their theories. The Golden Dawn exchanged Justice and strength to conform to the Jewish letters and correspondents.

4) with archetypal images such as tarot cards, it is not too difficult to see an esoteric system as similar to another system.

In 1778 Court De Gébelin and Count de Mellet were the first to suggest a link between the Tarot and the Cabal, and this was collected and expanded by Lévi, an occultist with dubious research skills. But because of Levi's high reputation in the magical world of that era, the association between Tarot and Cabal was simply considered a fact from that moment on, without anyone worrying about whether he was right or not.

Number 10

Elementary associations with the four seeds are another subsequent invention of the occultists and are not part of the original concept of tarot cards. Eliphas Lévi gave to Tarot the associations that are still accepted in most Tarot books today: batons / wands = fire; coins / Pentacles = Earth; cups = water; Swords = air.

Conclusion: tarot evolution is an information puzzle with pieces from scattered directions, and is derived from many cultures and many minds.

When you think about tarot cards, I would like you to remember that there are two main types of tarot decks, and they are very far apart from each other. We have historical Tarot, which was simply designed as a card game, and now we have modern Tarot, which was derived from and evolved from historical Tarot. The first tarot cards do not have mystical or magical qualities associated with it. The historical Tarot was an invention of the 15th century and was based on the cultural and historical and religious expressions of its time-nothing more, nothing less.

Modern Tarot has esoteric and mystical associations, but only because it was placed there in recent centuries, not because it is related to some ancient source of secret knowledge. To write all this, I'm not trying to belittle the Tarot or its heritage. I'm just trying to add a rational voice to the irrational accounts that some people think of passing as the "story" of tarot cards.

Modern Tarot has become a powerful set of mystical images that can legitimately be seen as a spiritual journey. It is full of magical, esoteric symbols and archetypes, making it a playground for the imagination. That's great! This is an important part of the place of the Tarot in today's world. However, when people promote a fictional story simply to heighten a subject's mystique, it undermines the value of its true nature when the truth is finally revealed.

The true history of the evolution of the Tarot is just as interesting as the factories. The original version may not look as magical or mysterious as its counterpart, but it is still fascinating. When you see an article that tells about the "mysterious and dark" origins of tarot cards, please delve deeper; you will find that the author did not bother to do serious research on the subject.

Tarot Cards for Beginners

While tarot cards can pale to play a normal deck, enjoying a whopping seventy-eight different cards, any beginner can get a pack and start practicing if they understand the fundamentals. The cards in the tarot pack can be divided into several categories:

Adapt

Main and smaller Arcanes

Pip Card

Court Documents

Once you understand the different characteristics of any category, reading tarot cards is simply a matter of mixing and matching information.

The most basic distribution of Tarot Cards is between the twenty-two main Arcanes, forty pip cards, and sixteen Court cards. The best way to begin to understand the meaning of each card is to arrange each of the 22 main Arcana in a circle, with the first card in position twelve. From there, looking through the map clockwise, you will be able to follow the path of the soul inevitably passes during its existence.

Around the first circle, then place forty pip cards. It begins with a Pentacles suit, the first twelve-position map depicting the winter solstice. In the position of three, follow the Pentacles suit with a sword suit, indicating the spring equinox. Then place the wand suit in a six-hour position, which means the summer solstice. Finally, it ends with a suite of Cups, starting with the position of the nine and marking the autumn equinox. Just as the rotation of the main Arcana represents a cycle, the rotation of the PIP map demonstrates the movement of the Earth around the sun through the seasons.

Finally, between these two circles, evenly distribute the remaining sixteen Court cards, working from the princess to the king in the seeds that correspond to the outer circle. These maps show different important personalities and how we grow over the years.

In this exercise, it is important to note that just because one card fell into the upper circle or the lower part is not more important than the other. Each card, whether it's major arcana or Minor Arcana, has a very special place in tarot reading.

Each seed in a smaller Arcane has very specific meanings that play an integral role in reading.

Cups: the cups are connected to the water element. Just as water can flow smoothly, be stopped by the dam, or boil and anger in the storm, as well as our emotions. When reading the cards that fall under the cups, it is important to read the procedure from one to ten in an emotional way.

Chopsticks: the chopsticks are attached to the fire element. Fire full of rhythm and movement; it can create and destroy. Therefore, chopsticks are the germ of change and action. Reading this dress, you will see cards that represent the first steps in a new beginning, the creation of our destiny, and cards that tell us that we acted too quickly, without thinking about the future.

Pentacle: Pentacles are associated with the element earth. The Earth is stable, solid, grounded. This is where we build our homes, feed ourselves, and support ourselves. Similarly, these dresses focus on the body and our senses. Whether it's creating a family environment where you feel safe, getting financial security, or taking care of yourself and building a family, all this will be found, if you read the pentacles.

Swords: swords are connected to the air element. We can't live without air, and we can't breathe. However, the air can also take your breath away in an instant. Just as the air can be sharp and pungent, so can the sword. This dress focuses on the intellect. It was said that there is no greater weapon than words, so beware of the warning that this seed can carry in terms of communication with others. It also explores the need for mental clarity and new ideas.

It also takes into account the personalities represented in the court's documents. These cards are incredibly important in reading because they can be directly related to you or someone who is closely related to your situation. Sometimes, it can help us understand who we can turn to for help, or who could hinder our progress.

Princesses: princesses and pages are interchangeable, and your deck will certainly be one or the other, but never both. When you draw a princess, you read about someone who is somehow young. Perhaps they have unfulfilled and unrecognized potential or are, in fact, a child. A princess can mean a student or someone who has just started a new adventure in her life.

Princes: princes are synonymous with Knights in a tarot reading, and again the bridge will have one or the other, but never both. The principles symbolize movement and action; they thirst for progress in life and can often be naively idealistic. People who are read like a prince are warned about actions without thinking because they often jump the gun and assume that everything will work out in the best case. Princes are considered eager in all things and are a generous type of person who is always eager to help others.

Queens are considered caring and intuitive people. They are highly respected and admired and lead inspiration rather than command. The Queen can represent a man or a woman if it is someone who illustrates the above aspects. Often, they are a mature person or a relative- someone with life experience to draw on when offering advice.

Kings represent a person who grew up in his life and is now wise and perfect. Often the person who is represented by this card will feel a great duty and responsibility towards others, placing the needs of friends and family before their own.

After examining the classifications of court cards, seeds, and how to arrange a set of tarot cards in order to trace its history, the meaning of each card should begin to become clear. At this time, a beginner could choose a deck card and give it at least a very simple definition. Once you feel comfortable with this information, consider the numbers from one to ten and finally go through all the main mysterious cards one by one. When you have an understanding of what each number represents, and what the titles of the major arcanes represent, you can then read tarot de Marseille. It will take practice, and sometimes, you may need to refer to the reference table, but slowly and surely understand the concepts that go into the divisions of tarot cards, and everyone can pick up and be a simple and basic tarot reader.

Make your Own Tarot Card Deck

A Tarot card game is something that many people want to use, but I do not know which formula to choose. The number of tarot games available can be surprising to some. And while you might like a few tarot card games, you may not be able to afford more than one. Instead of wasting time looking at the tarot decks available, it's time to make your own tarot deck exactly to your specifications.

You will need some supplies before making a tarot pack for you. To begin with, you need a thicker quality paper on which you can make drawings of Tarot. If you find a paper with a pattern on one side and an empty area on the other, everything is better. Take this paper and cut it into 78 corresponding squares or rectangles, to your liking. Then collect artistic needs to create drawings on the empty side of the paper. Things like markers and colored pencils are ideal because they do not rub.

If you want to imitate the ideas of a traditional tarot card pack, you will want to look for a real tarot card pack or a card online. This way, you can start with an idea for each card, but you can create your own unique patterns. Look at the examples of tarot as simply inspiration; it does not have pictures that you need to copy. For example, you can make a five-stroke, but the chopsticks can look as you like, and there may be other background images you call.

Finally, to complete the package, you need to create a safe place to stay when it is not in use. You can buy a box or bag that can be used to store your cards, for example. And then you can decorate this box or bag to help you make this room something more personal and special. Some people also choose to laminate their cards to add a layer of protection and stability.

Regardless of your reasons for wanting a tarot, remember that you do not need to spend a lot of money or even adhere to "traditional" models. To see the future, you can start with the cards created by your own hands.

How to Predict the Future Using a Tarot Deck

Is it possible to predict the future? What about the Tarot deck? Yes, it is! Read on, and you'll find out how.

Extract your favorite tarot pack or fortune teller. It is better to stay in a quiet space, but the most important thing is to work with cards. All these are amazing tools that can help create a contemplative atmosphere. It works best with a tarot card or Oracle decks, asking open questions rather than yes/no questions. Some open question tips are listed below. Yes/no question would be how to tear off daisy's petals, "does she love me? Or don't you like me?"I have a raise."

What kind of energy will I have to monitor in July?

My annual exam is scheduled for the last week of March. What areas of improvement will be discussed in my review?

I'm going to propose to my girlfriend. What is the most favorable Week and day to ask her?

My son is starting a new school. What energy do we need to know about his school? Will the change make him succeed?

Tomorrow is Monday, what kind of energy do I meet at work? House? On the highway?

Take your time, formulate, and explore each question. Make sure the question is exactly what you want to know. Vague questions will give you vague and often frustrating answers. An example of a vague question can be: "why can't I find a good job? Instead, you might ask, "What kind of energy do I have to get a better job?"

After formulating and considering your question on the day you wanted education, take the Tarot platform (or Oracle platform). Mix the cards and think about your question. Download the map. Meditate on the map. Note the story that the map tells you or the story that makes you think. It could be Little Red Riding Hood, or Uncle Ted came across a piece of wildflower. History does not matter, neither real nor fictitious. Look at the colors and what they represent for you. Look at the numbers, the time, the symbols you see on the maps. Do not forget about the traditions of Tarot meanings.

During meditation, focus on the map of the symbol, shape, or color that represents the shapes of the map. Let the shape, symbol, color dance in your head until you form the next one. In the calendar, write it or draw it and all other information you received. Do not judge the information that comes. Write down what it is. The image of a ship sinking in the Blood Red Sea may not mean a real wreck. It could be a prediction that the 15th day In January of next year, the company you work for may have a huge drop in the price of their shares and are left in the red financially. Pay attention to everything, regardless of whether it makes sense or not.

To what extent it is necessary to request information in the future. If you want to know about next week or about seven months in the future, it doesn't matter. Tradition says not to ask more than six months in advance, because the energy around the event, the person, etc. can change. However, the same applies to any reading. Two hours later, energy could change for up to two decades in the future.

If you have received forecast-based information, you should consider reconnecting to maps a week or a month before the forecast date. People change their minds, learn new skills, and someone may die, they can become all sorts of things that can affect time. Whether something changes or not, you have a strong answer. If things are completely different, you can find out what new energies will affect that day.

Be vigilant for cards, labels, symbols, colors, etc. that are repeated in each of your predictive data. The more something is repeated, the more news it is.

If you read about other people, pay attention to the repetition in the cards; if you see one or more cards, it repeats again and again, regardless of the person reading. This occurs mainly for four to six months. Attention. If a map of the tower appears at each reading, this could mean another collapse of the bank. If the moon appears, it could mean that we have an emotional turn for the event. In either case, a map or not a map, this repetition means that change is coming. Something is happening socially, politically, or economically.

Start predicting your future, pull up the calendar, or turn on the phone. Extract any tool to maintain a normal life. Using tarot cards or Oracle decks, you can predict the future.

RWS Tarot - A Brief Introduction

The Rider Waite Smith Tarot deck is probably the most popular and well known of all tarot decks that are available today. The name comes from William RIDER & son-the original editor, Arthur Edward WAITE-the academic and mystic who commissioned the creation of this game, and Pamela Colman SMITH-the talented but often neglected artist, who drew pictures from the Rider-Waite Tarot game (as it is often called). Waite and Smith were both members of the Order of Golden Dawn, the famous but fleeting occult group of the 19th century.

RWS tarot card game was released in 1909 and was the first widely available game with illustrated minor arcane cards. Fifty-six tiny arcane cards, also known as "pecks," today had a wealth of symbolism displayed in the pictures, as well as twenty-two major mysterious cards. Until then, less mysterious cards on the tarot deck showed only four cups, or six chopsticks or eight swords. RWS tarot cards with illustrated "pips," as well as evocative images of the main Arcana, finally revolutionize the world of tarot cards. When Waite designed his tarot package, he maintained a basic sequence of cards, even as he changed card numbering and fairness in the main Arcanes. There is debate about who actually designed the minor Arcane cards. It was said that Waite designed and gave Smith full instructions or just told her your thoughts and gave free rein to their artistic talents to create images. Each card carries a monogram of Pamela Colman Smith, usually in one of the lower corners.

The original print of the albums was tragically destroyed in the London bombing, and the release ended. In 1971, US Games Inc. he began publishing a protected fax version of the game.

These days, many bridges follow the basic pattern of the RWS tarot deck. There are RW versions that were re-colored, but kept on designs of this original line. Versions that have been redesigned usually have the same basic numbers and parameters on maps with similar symbolism. Game type RWS is generally recommended for beginners, because the basic visual scenes may be more easily associated with keywords, to make it easier to memorize and understand the meaning of each card. However, there are also many experienced readers whose favorite reading platform is an RWS or variant. Most books for beginners and beginners use illustrations of the RWS bridge for learning purposes.

One thing is certain, if Arthur Edward Waite and Pamela Colman Smith didn't have to work together to create a tarot deck-RWS tarot would be very different from what we are accustomed to today.

Waite Tarot - Information About Waite Tarot

Waite Tarot is one of the most popular existing card games. Card reading has been around for a long time. People turn to the prediction of the future to get answers to their most desired questions. In 1909, A. email. Waite created his famous cards and was issued by the rider company, thus getting the name of The Rider-Waite Tarot card. There are a lot of articles about tarot cards and reading outside, so I'll talk about the meaning of the inverted card.

Each time, when the player mixes cards, some of them end upside down; for beginners, it is recommended to ignore it and turn it in the right direction. Once the newcomer has gained experience, he should start paying attention to the inverted card. Everyone knows that each Waite Tarot card symbolizes certain energy, and when the reading of the Cards is carried out, the energy collection gives the answer to the researcher. It is commonly known that cards collect energy when mixed and cut. Energy is of a different nature; some are strong, others are weak, others stay in your life, some leaves, as the energies are distributed, you decide the exact situation.

Every time you act on a vertical card, then its energy is free to manifest itself, the characteristics, which contains the Waite Tarot card, are readily available and active, but when we deal with inverted cards, the energy is not fully developed. It can be considered that it is in the early stages or loses energy, is incomplete, or even unavailable. The features of these maps are present, but they cannot be expressed completely.

It is a good idea that you keep track of how many cards you deal vertically and how many upside down. If most Cards are straight, then your energies are free and strong. In this case, the purpose is clear. If the opposite happens, then you have little energy, and the goal is tarnished. If energies are not freely developed, they go wherever they want.

Waite Tarot Cards are a great tool for contact with the energies around us. Life is an endless flow of energy; when a person understands this flow and uses it creatively, then anything will be possible. We should not pretend that inverted cards add a different aspect of your value, and this helps you better interpret Waite Tarot cards.

Tarot Cards Spread

Tarot Cards are distributed differently depending on the questions you want to find answers to. The spread of the Celtic cross is popular because it responds to many aspects, including the current condition of the person, past events, affecting the present, and a possible future that may or may not occur. Dissemination of reports is another common spread, and it reveals the current status of her report, the way the message is controlled, and what aspects of the report should be considered.

Other spreads include astrological, Planetarium, Tetraktys, Cross and Triangle, Mandala, star guide, Tree of life, past, life, and dream spread.

For centuries, people depended on reading tarot cards and palms to predict future events. Gifted persons carried out these data for a fee. The practice is still present in today's modern world, and many people still consult the reader. The beliefs of those who go for reading vary greatly. Some believe in an unchanging fate and use the information to prepare themselves to face everything that happens to them.

Others use the information to make the right choice. These people and entrepreneurs usually occupy positions of responsibility. They want to know the consequences of their actions and the impact of their decisions on their performance. Despite the goals of physical reading, practice is gaining great popularity in society.

What tarot cards are on the market

Many types of tarot cards are available on the market. When mixed, form a pattern on the surface, such as a table. The template is tarot spreads, and each tarot reader has its favorite templates. As with many professions, when a new person begins to work, he must start with simple basic tasks. New Tarot readers should start with simple tarot cards. Deviations differ in the number of cards in the range. Simple deviations include five to one card. The rest includes between six and all cards in the tarot package.

What determines the deviations of the tarot card

The type of spread of tarot cards depends on the questions to which the client wants to answer. Some popular models are suitable for certain questions, and depending on the specific needs of the customer. Reading tarot cards is not difficult to read. The requirement of the reader is the concentration and ability to interpret the meaning of different patterns of Tarot multiplication. This requires great cognitive abilities and memorizing skills.

The simplest scatter is the scatter of three cards. The player mixes the deck, then divides it into three piles. Then the reader takes the card from each pile and puts it on the table with his face. The reader should keep the question in mind during all these activities and focus on the answer. The map on the left side of the tray presents a history question, while the map in the center is associated with the current events surrounding the question. The last card on the right represents the possible future of the problem.

Another extension of tarot cards for beginners is the spread of tarot cards with four cards. To interpret this, the reader mixes the cards with the question in mind. Then the player takes four cards from the top of the deck and spreads them on the table face down and from left to right. The first tarot card from left to right represents the past, the second present, and the third Future of the application. The fourth card is the answer to the question.

Tarot Myth Busters

The purpose of this book is to try to clarify obsolete and unnecessary superstitions related to reading Tarot cards.

Ask all experienced and ethical readers of tarot cards, if they believe that tarot cards are bad, the work of the devil, and only psychics and clairvoyants can read them, they can leave with a laugh. I would have done the same thing. The more I use and work with these cards, the more I understand their true meaning and capabilities.

When using cards with a group of people who claim to have no knowledge of tarot cards, it is always fascinating to hear the answer when the death card spins. A strong hold of breath is, to put it mildly, a whisper: "Oh, death!'. Everyone was sitting at the table, do not mislead us, that I really did not understand the death map; they were led to believe the wrong meaning for this map and more. Then what happens is that eventually, I will explain the correct meaning and convince them of this fact, with the impression that they prefer the drama of the original meaning.

Most cards are made of wood pulp and Printing Ink, created in card shapes with an image on one side and a pattern on the back, all 78 cards. Which is exactly what they are and everything they will ever be. Even digital images are just a display of the image of symbols and works of art. It is the meaning that is the most interesting part.

Tarot has evolved over the centuries, with their history perhaps starting from 15 playing cards. A century, maybe even earlier. Their development as a divination tool is not very clear, but many use a lot of elements as a tool in the future, including; throwing animal bones, chicken entrails, throwing dice, runes, consuming drugs from plants, looking into a bowl of water, plus the elegant art of drinking cup, sometimes I used cappuccino foam and I know beer is used too.

Hollywood is also responsible for many myths today; the meaning of the devil's map has been edited so that it is abused to show the real death in the film. It is a cheap supplement to add atmosphere and fear. Tarot readers are depicted as the mysterious companion, dressed in flowing clothes, with turbans, excessive jewelry, and bad taste; actors are without exception depicted as gypsy fortune-tellers in a tent or caravan with a crystal ball on the table. It's about showcases and hammers.

Superstition around the Tarot is a work of fiction, perhaps built by people who want to add mystery and control; they can fabricate an idea that they have special mastery, secret knowledge, and gifts. It is an attraction to hide their insecurity. If the tarot reader is good, he has nothing to prove, word of mouth will be enough. The wardrobe of unusual clothes is the last thing that a decent Tarot card needs to increase its reputation.

Most superstitions are quite recent, in the last century, gained momentum with the advent of cinema, television, and a significant increase in the number of people interested in Tarot. These myths also increased in volume and were heavily embroidered along the way.

We distract the most popular:

You should never buy your own tarot cards.

If that were the case, I would still be waiting for my first card game. I don't know why or where it started; it doesn't make sense. This is a very good thing, who else will know exactly what style of cards you like or "talk?" Enjoy looking at the different styles in bookstores and online, ask to see friends, maps, valuable research, and collection of different Tarot decks. In the end, you can design your own.

Never Let Others Touch Your Tarot Cards.

I understand that someone is very special and does not like all Tom, Dick, or Harry to manipulate your cards, but nothing bad will happen if others touch your deck. I've been using the same board for over 12 years, and it made me proud, when someone asks to look at their cards, they often expect me to refuse, but I'm happy to go on and explain a little bit about them. I'll stir it up. This is the perfect time to ask questions and clarify some myths.

Only fortune tellers can read tarot cards.

Yes, clairvoyants can read tarot cards, especially if they have studied them, and the same applies to everyone, we can all read them. Some people understand the cards and can read them without any exercise, but most of us will have to work. Is it possible that we all learned to read tarot cards, whether we have the right books, or/and an online course, another tarot card, which teaches us how; we all need a place to start. Enriches tarot reading, if the reader is psychic, clairvoyant and/or intuitive, there are professional readers, who do not qualify for any of the previous characteristics, but studied and practiced, until he becomes more than competent.

The purpose of this article is to try to clarify the obsolete and unnecessary superstitions associated with reading Tarot cards.

The above answer also applies to doctors, psychologists, police officers, military, and people in business, you know, they read maps. There is a package for everyone; hundreds of tarot styles, from Egyptian Arthurian, fairies, Lord of the Rings; go online and see for yourself. Outside, someone is working on their own deck of cards. There is also someone out there looking for enlightenment, advice, inner wisdom as they shuffle their tarot cards. It's for everyone. Why do witches have fun?

Tarot Cards are magical.

No, absolutely not. They are manufactured, packaged, and shipped wholesale or stored. I'm sorry if I ruined everything for you. They are used as a reading tool, symbols, meanings, and images that trigger the flow of information. Look at them as they are and avoid myths.

Tarot Cards are bad.

Tarot cards do not have magical properties or bad qualities; they are just Cards. All decent Tarot readers will use the cards to help, enlighten, show alternative options, answer questions, in a variety of good and useful ways. They would never have thought of doing it differently. Anyone who claims to use them for evil purposes is mistaken and deceives others.

We have not heard of the cards accused of wrongdoing.

The Gypsies Invented The Tarot.

There is no evidence that the Gypsies played a role in the development of tarot cards. Tarot has evolved from a deck of cards to the 15th century or earlier, in Europe, with the use of expensive, hand-painted gifts ordered by aristocrats, to serially produced woodcuts for the public to buy.

Tarot Cards Are Never Wrong.

Tarot Cards are used to illuminate the paths and options you have in your life, options, and alternatives. The future is not in the stone, but the sand, it's up to you, the future of the road you take, there may be a little more detours along the road, you will probably end up in the same place. Free will and choice to play an important role in your life and tarot cards can reflect this.

Tarot Cards Come From Egypt

These rumors and scams began with the trial of Gebelin. He misinterpreted two Egyptian words, believing that they had an average Tarot, and it was only when the rosette Stone was translated after 1799 that his error was clear.

Tarot cards cannot be read by phone

Of course, they can, it is as simple as the client asks the question, and the Tarot reader then writes the question, shuffles the cards and continues to read. This also applies to reading on the internet; this is the same technique. Just because this person, the querent, is not sitting next to you, does not mean that you cannot interact and give them answers with the help of tarot cards. Sometimes, I would type the answer and print it or email it, and it's just as valid.

Cats Will Undermine Your Skill.

When it was first suggested, my jaw took. Needless to say, I invited the four cats in the family to read that night. God knows where it started. That is not a piece of truth.

Pregnant Women Should Not Read Cards

If this were true, health warnings would be printed on the sides of card packs. It is absolutely safe for pregnant women to read the cards; they may be able to level the cards on their bump as they do.

You Can't Read Tarot Cards.

Yes, of course, you can, but first, write a question on paper and use a tarot book that you believe for answers. The trick is to use the answer books on the cards for your answer; otherwise, you can find the fight unbiased or detached. By writing all this, you can check so late.

You don't want anyone to read it, and it's a method for development.

Your tarot cards should be wrapped in silk.

Only if you like silk, I use old silk scarves that are loved and difficult to separate; this prevents the edge of the paper from scratches. In addition, it is a joy to the touch. As for my "working" platform, which lives in a gadget bag, usually purchased to protect and carry MP3 players. Two bridges and a digital recorder can fit into it. No one knows what's inside when I wear it.

Tarot Cards Are The Work Of The Devil.

Of course not. They are the work of people who want to help others, help them with the problems they have, improve their lives, discover new techniques for taking responsibility, use modern psychology. Many of these people are professional classes, doctors, psychologists, psychiatrists, nurses, scientists, consultants, etc. what circulates, happens.

The Cards Are Hidden

The word occultism means hidden. We know that the cards came from playing cards in the 15th of the XIX century, with different groups interested in them and attaching their own beliefs and meanings. The word occult has been used over the years, trying to give a false view of their true use and suggesting something wrong.

Death Map Means Death

Simply put, it means change. If you want to change careers and this map will appear in one reading, you can feel a huge sense of relief, depending on whether you know the true meaning. It's a map that filmmakers use to suggest that there will be an evil death without really appreciating what they are doing. Therefore, Tarot readers spend a lot of time reassuring their clients when this card appears. Change.

Not all tarot readers can be trusted

I can be prejudiced if I answer this! Always stick to the word when looking for someone to give you a reading. Any profession can have a charlatan, a cheater, or a woman. Just a little patience and make sure that the Tarot reader is well thought out. If you are reading and you feel very unhappy with the way things are going, make a quick exit. Ideally, you should have a feeling of well-being after reading, a feeling of clarification, do not feel like you are flying blind. Use your instincts.

Reverse Cards Are Always Terrible.

Some people choose not to use inverted cards during the game so that it sticks to 78 vertical meanings. This means you're going to lose another 78 meanings, and some of them are very, very positive. This simply means studying a little more as you learn, I suggest you look at some tarot books on online bookstores that have the best-inverted Tarot meanings. This will expand your knowledge and reading.

Top Ten Myths about Tarot Cards and Tarot Reading

Myth 1 - "Tarot cards can predict the future."

Predicting the future is not difficult; we can all do it. For example, if you know someone who constantly spends more than it earns and pays for it by building up the debts of credit cards, then it is not hard to predict where he's going. Or, if you know someone who is expecting a baby, you can count on experience, accurately predict that they have many months of lack of sleep and fatigue in advance. Tarot cards do a little more. It has centuries of human experience distilled into a simple philosophy and meaning of each paper. Another way of looking at it is to say that the tarot cards do not make precise predictions of the future, simply allow us to catch a glimpse of some of the likely possibilities.

Myth 2 - "tarot cards come from ancient Egypt."

The first that tarot cards can be dated is the 16th century in Italy. There is no evidence that Tarot exists anywhere else in the world. Some people claim that the cards come from India or China, but this is also baseless speculation.

Myth 3 - "Acceptance of the death card means that someone dies."

Likely. The point of the symbolism of the Cards is that they represent deeper truths than life. Taking all the cards literally would lose layers of meaning and intuition. In the case of the death map of the medieval spirit, death represented an inevitable change and often a journey to a better place. The Charter represents change and evolution. However, the possibility that this sometimes means death cannot be ruled out.

Myth 4 - "Reading the pleasure of Tarot in the occultism."

There are many claims that the tarot cards have pagan, witchcraft, or shamanic roots, and some even involve tarot cards in devil worship and satanic rituals. Another common claim is that the tarot cards originated from ancient religions now forgotten. None of this is true. Tarot cards, as already mentioned, originate from medieval Italy, and the predominant cultural context of that time was Christian. The symbolism of the Cards is Christian or Jewish-A New Testament or an old one. The word "occult" means" hidden," so, in this sense, you can say that reading has something to do with magic because you are trying to reveal what is hidden.

Myth 5 - "Reading your cards will bring bad luck."

Professional readers and those experienced with cards know that it is not true, but this is often repeated. This may stem from the fact that Tarot readers avoid reading their cards. Not because she's unlucky, but because she's not effective. A good tarot reading requires three parts; the questioner, the reader, and the bridge. The reader tries to remain objective and reports to the questioner what the cards say, without any bias or desire to hear a specific message. Playing this role for your reading is difficult, if not impossible.

Myth 6 - "You must have a certain psychic ability to read tarot cards."

Most people can learn to read tarot cards to a smaller or larger extent. No psychic power is needed because all wisdom is in Maps and meanings that have been developed over the years. Actually, if we were psychics, why would you use Tarot Cards? Tarot works best when the reader drops his prejudices and feelings on the problem and leaves only the cards to speak.

Myth 7 - "No one should ever worry about their tarot package."

Some interns do not allow anyone else to touch their tarot cards. Even if they read something, they won't let the interview mix the game up on their own. In my experience, this valuable attitude comes from those who want to build themselves, and their platform will be something special. Let me see what you want. This is contrary to the spirit of the Tarot, which promotes open investigation and sharing of understanding. Allowing customers to shuffle cards helps them feel part of the process and focus on the problem in hand.

Myth 8 "Tarot cards can be used to cast spells or perform other people."

Sometimes it is considered that tarot cards can be used to keep things moving rather than predicting. To influence someone's life from afar, for good or evil. It is very far from what cards are actually, which is simple to understand. There is no reason to believe that tarot cards have a different power than intuition. One of the frequent messages based on the tarot data is, in fact, a bad ability that sometimes we have to influence our lives without talking about someone else. Just to give a tarot would probably say: "Get a grip before you try to change others."

Myth 9 - "Different bridges provide different figurines."

It's a little subjective, but not in my experience. Regardless of the bridge, the meanings obtained during the four centuries remain the same. However, different people will refer more strongly to some of the bridges, rather than the other, and the images with which the client is more comfortable to create the best atmosphere for reading. A cynical person may suspect that this myth is multiplied by the creators of bridges.

Myth 10 - "It's dangerous to have too much data on tarot cards."

There is a belief that people who become obsessed with tarot cards and continue to make one after the second reading, you're out of luck, or take a risk, push yourself over the limit. Perhaps it is true that the search for permanent help can be a sign of an impending crisis. These people could still be near the edge. The main thing is that too many tips hurt anyone and lead only to confusion.

Know All About Your Love Life Through Love Tarot Reading

Love and emotions can cloud judgments and leave you confused. It can affect other aspects of your life and get you down.

It is better to clarify issues related to love, relationship, and progress in life.

Tarot provides meaningful answers and directions to define your situation and what you can do to change the situation for the better.

Formulate specific questions and problems before going for a love tarot reading

Interestingly, experienced and gifted Tarot readers first find out what exactly your interest is and what your questions are when you approach them for the love tarot reading.

Then it exposes the number of cards in a template.

In general, you can question classified information as relating to you, love, and your love life in the future, how to find love, how to resolve conflicts, and to spread the love of the couple.

For each type, the medium tarot reader will spread the cards in a special way and invent the love of reading.

Tarot Love Spreads

In a love tarot reading, the reader can take advantage of specific spreads, which usually defines the relationship Tarot deviations, such as finding love to spread, love bottom line spread, relationship deviations, and couple reading deviations. The number of Cards selected can vary from five to twelve.

Your friendly Tarot reader will arrange tarot cards according to the problem. Then each card is read for its individual interpretation and relative to other cards that appear in the span. Each card has a related question. For example, the first card may concern why you are still free. The second card shows you how to overcome this situation, and the third card will inform you about the positive aspect of your potential partner.

An example is the Empress's card. If it happens in your spread and stands, it represents the result, and its symbol is Venus, showing positive developments are in stock in the near future. In itself, it means one thing. The Tarot reader interprets the card, your question, and other cards, and comes up with a detailed answer.

In case the problems with love and relationship bother you, contact the tarot expert to read the Tarot of love.

Knowing your wishes, the Tarot reader will arrange the game in a special way specifically for the love tarot reading session that gives you the long-awaited answers.

Using the Tarot to Find Love

Undoubtedly, the most common survey when reading tarot is about love. It often seems that true love is something that is outside of yourself; it is the external force or the act of Destiny over which we have little control. In fact, the search for love begins with ourselves. Love is a Genesis that manifests itself in our inner beings. A happy and successful relationship begins with ourselves.

The best relationships are those in which both partners find out who they are. When a person develops with a strong sense of self, his partnership will most likely blossom. With self-consciousness, a person is more able to express his feelings and establish appropriate boundaries. They know their own needs and the needs of their partners. Above all, for someone who is single, can recognize the qualities of a potential partner that will work or not.

In the individual tarot tips on Love Matters, Most Tarot readers and psychics tend to focus directly on the current energy of someone's love life. They often do not realize the influence of their own systems of belief or behavior. During a tarot reading, it is really up to the individual to ask the tarot reader or psychic to explore the topic of their level of personal development and how it can affect their love life. A good tarot reader can read it immediately. Love problems must change their orientation. Instead of asking when I would find love? Try to explore the areas that prevent you from finding love. Here are some questions that can be very useful during a love tarot reading.

1. Where are the areas I need to grow to find love?

2. What's keeping me from finding love?

3. What do I need to know about myself so that I can meet a partner?

4. What are my behaviors that affect my love life?

5. What should I think of love?

6. What areas should I change?

7. Where can I not talk?

8. What do I have to do to open myself to love?

The more you learn about yourself, the more likely you will meet the perfect love. It is important to remember that when a person uses tarot for love, tarot serves as a seer. Tarot reading is a tool of self-renewal and growth. In truth, Tarot is a tool that is available to all who wish to explore their own inner workings. This is an incredibly effective method of immersing ourselves in the deepest areas of ourselves that affect our current relationships. Tarot data will never reveal our secrets that remain out of sight.

Tarot reading serves as a guide. They are mirrors that reflect our truths. When it comes to love, tarot cards can lead us to the manifestation of our goals and dreams. They reveal our vulnerabilities and the areas that prevent us from flourishing. In a love tarot card, you can find out what affects us and highlights situations that we may have been aware of. Above all, Tarot offers us a new sense of awareness of who we are. In the end, a tarot reading can open us to love.

As for love, there is nothing like a good tarot reading. Tarot cards offer a unique perspective that illuminates the nature of our relationships. I am here to guide you on your journey, both personally and romantic. Questions about love are by far the most common questions asked when reading the tarot. However, many people are disappointed or dissatisfied. The cause of this is often the questions that are asked. The most important aspect of successful tarot reading is to ask the right questions.

The most common mistake that is made when reading the tarot is the preservation of information. People do this when they question or test the ability of a tarot reader. It is quite normal to worry when working with a new tarot reader, especially if this is the first time you will receive a reading. In these circumstances, the biggest problem is the lack of openness of mind. Unfortunately, you do not need this or that tarot reader. The retention of information can ultimately disrupt the ability of the Tarot reader.

When you get a tarot reading, the best approach is to stay open to your questions about love prepared before you start reading. A professional tarot reader understands the cards and has learned to interpret their meaning. The more accurate you will be with a tarot reader, the better it will be able to help you read. Take the time to justify yourself with doubts and let yourself be guided by the cards. You will be surprised at the amount of information you can receive when you stay recipient.

The best questions to ask at first reading love tarot should not be in black and white. In other words, asking if someone you love or if your relationship will work can give the Tarot reader very little work. Here are some examples of open-ended questions that might be useful when reading Tarot a message.

1. What affects my relationship?

2. What is touching my interest in love now?

3. How could I develop this relationship?

4. What should I understand about myself?

5. What should I understand about my interest in love?

6. What is the potential outcome of this report?

7. What should I do to bring a romantic relationship into my life?

The list can go on, and you can be as creative as you want. Asking carefully planned questions can lead to very rewarding tarot readings.

It is also wise to inform the Tarot reader about the context of your situation. This is especially true for the tarot details of love. By allowing the Tarot reader to fully understand the nature of your situation, the more they will be able to guide you. The history of the situation often improves the Reading of tarot cards. This gives the reader a broader perspective and allows him to understand the problems he is facing. It also lets you know what has affected your relationship.

Finally, it is important to remember that a good Tarot reader will never tell you what to do. They are essentially messengers. You are your master, and you have your free will. You have the power to choose your own paths and behaviors. When it comes to love, you are always the best guide. While tarot readings can often reveal important influences, they still have the power to make their own decisions and choose their own plan of action.

How to Get an Accurate Love Tarot Reading

How do you better read love tarot cards? This is an important question because most people who ask to read love tarot cards end up confused or disappointed after reading it. Yet questions about love, relationships, marriage, divorce, and soul mates remain the most frequently asked questions in reading.

The most common mistake that people make when consulting with a psychic card reader or tarot cards about love and relationships is to keep the information for the purpose of testing the reader. If you are skeptical about tarot cards, do not waste your money reading. This act of non-supply can lead to incorrect values and can be easily confused.

A good love tarot reader will know how to interpret the cards to personalize the reading for the querent before them so that the specific questions that you have about your love and relationships can be specified exactly. Since there are many ways to interpret maps, the more information provided to the reader, the more accurate the reading.

Here's an example. If you want to know if your partner is cheating on you or not, ask this question, rather than "is there another man/woman in his life?" In the life of a man, there are always other women and another man in the life of a woman. Maybe they're not in love. In a love tarot reading, an important person can appear in such cards as a father, brother, close friend.

This does not necessarily mean infidelity. The reader needs some information to interpret the cards specifically to your situation because different cards can have different meanings. The context in which the questions were asked, the placement in the spread of tarot cards, as well as the reader's intuition contribute to getting a good reading of love tarot cards. Be very specific about all the questions you have about your love from the very beginning. If you want to know whether or not you should be with your current love, ask this question rather than a lot of questions around the main problem.

Ask me, "what if I stay? What happens if I leave? Will I be happy if I stay? Will anything change if I stick to it?" These questions will give you the real answers you need to help you solve your problems with love and relationship.

Often a tarot reader can leave out important information that appears in the cards if you strictly focus on the question you asked when you have a lot. So, give the big picture at the beginning and all your questions so that you can get the best possible reading tarot love, and you will not be disappointed.

Love Tarot Reading and the Devil Tarot Card

Perhaps one of the scariest cards for reading love tarot is the devil's card. The image of the devil raises fear, uncertainty, and concern. However, in most love tarot figures, The Devil's Tarot card is often misunderstood. The Devil's Tarot should not be interpreted literally. In fact, this is a metaphor for our behavior and attachment to other people. In love tarot readings, the devil acts as a messenger. Its appearance guarantees reflection and a willingness to explore our behavior towards others.

The meaning of the tarot card of the devil's Tarot card traditionally refers to the issues of materialism and egocentrism. This is a warning that you can abuse their energy or influence. It also refers to self-pity, and the insatiable need to fulfill one's most primitive desires. The devil is a Tarot card that forces you to enter their shadow and realize their darkest impulses. In the end, you need to cope with these impulses and learn to control them. The devil reminds us that if we are not informed of our behavior, we are slaves to them.

When reading tarot love, the devil's tarot cards often refer to their own emotional dependence on their romantic relationship. Basically, the Devil's Tarot card is a card of interdependence. When you become completely dependent on their partner, they lose their personal freedom. This kind of freedom comes in the form of inner independence: a person does not need to be chained to another person in order to feel whole and satisfied. Reading the Tarot of love, the devil may suggest that there are attachments that can greatly depend on the neighbor. The devil remembers that they have their own inner power and the ability to take care of you, whether they are in a relationship or not.

Another hint of the tarot card of the devil in love is his reference to past painful relationships. In this case, it is usually an unhealthy connection or a negative projection in their current relationship. The devil's map reminds us that man has become a slave to his past. Their romantic relationship can be affected by old wounds that have not been treated emotionally. The devil asks you to explore the nature of your current relationship. Now is the time to wonder if your relationship is healthy. Are you in bondage? Are you repeating past behavior? Is your relationship motivated by the needs of early childhood that have never been sufficiently met? Do you decide to stay in an unhealthy relationship because you are trying to heal old wounds?

In love tarot readings, the devil's Tarot card pushes you to become conscious. It is a map that guarantees attention and reflection. The devil wants us to look inside and study our impulses and needs. Are we slaves to them? If so, how can we free ourselves? When it comes to romantic relationships, the devil reminds us that we have the power to choose the relationships we want. It reminds us that we must be ready to face our past fears and wounds, to find personal freedom and integrity.

Love Tarot Reading and the Justice Card

When the Justice Tarot card appears in a love tarot reading, you can be sure that the issues of balance and equity affect your relationship. The tarot card of justice often indicates that the relationship may require overwork. It is necessary to achieve mutual understanding and acceptance in order to advance the relationship. This is often achieved through compromise, donation, and reception. When you read love tarot cards, the tarot card pushes you to use your emotions and think objectively. It's time you told your partner the truth.

Justice often appears in a love tarot reading When relationship cycles are nearing completion. That is, the relationship is at a crossroads, where it can hesitate or move forward in a new direction. Justice tells us that this is a moment of reflection, where the strengths and weaknesses of relations must be subjected to close control. Both partners must be responsible and take responsibility for their behavior and actions. Justice tells us that it's time to be honest and put things in order so that the relationship can grow and prosper. Or, otherwise, the relationship could be in serious danger.

If you find yourself in a desperate situation with your partner, do not feel discouraged, because the Charter of justice often indicates great changes in the relationship, this may be true. However, you are not yet aware of it. This can be a good time to reach out to your partner to express your concerns. Communication and attentive listening can have a huge impact on your relationship. Sharing your feelings can certainly encourage sincerity, openness, and integrity. When this is achieved, conflicts will occur much less, and old anxieties and tensions can be replaced by a new understanding and a New Balance found.

The disadvantage is that the Inverted Tarot card Justice may indicate that you are forced to make uncomfortable decisions, which is struggling with divorce, divorced, or custody issues. When reading, tarot love can reverse the Charter of Justice refer to a one-sided relationship or lack of balance between partners. There may be legal problems, or the relationship may be full of hatred, lack of responsibility, or a partner, who may be treating others unfairly. The reverse Charter of justice can also serve as a warning that you or your partner is too strict or categorical. In such cases, it is important that both partners are honest, open, and willing to work to find a solution.

Do not be discouraged too much if you cannot. Be honest with yourself and continue your actions, even if the situation you are experiencing is difficult. In the end, the decision you make will always be right if you stay honest.

Love Tarot Reading and the Magician Card

In love tarot readings, the Magician represents the elements of spells and magic that is found in our relationships. It represents the creative power behind attraction, love, and Union. His appearance in love tarot reading often means a period of mania and magnetism. This presence should justify the excitement and caution because the mage has an irregular nature, and the energy around him can be intense and powerful.

Traditionally, the Tarot card is a manifestation card. His reminder is that his ideas can be consolidated into a particular reality. The magician is an action card and learned to direct the divine energy into the physical plane. In other words, The Magician creates with the help of the divine. It is a conscious connection between the deity and the kingdom of man. It is a map of creation that shows its forces in the everyday world.

In love reading tarot, the magic of a magician can bring together two people. If you were looking for a new partnership, it would be time to put your creative energy to use and confidence in the process. The magician makes you feel the strength in you and recognize that you have the power to create your own reality. Using your own self-confidence can help you make important connections. If you are already in a relationship, then "magic is in the air" It's time to explore with your partner. Your joint efforts could yield lasting results.

In reading the tarot of love, a magician can also represent a significant love or other interest. The magician can also point to an individual who has learned to control the world around him in order to achieve his goals. He is a person who wants to stay active and constantly tries to make things move. He is a man who knows how to use his abilities to create the world he wants. It can be a beautiful speaker and adaptable to any situation you are in.

A negative element of the magician of Tarot Cards is his vulnerability to cheating. In this regard, it can be false or lead to false intentions. When tarot figures appear in love, he always represents a person you need to know before you give him your heart.

Love tarot Reading and the Sun Card

In love tarot readings, The Sun Tarot card is the card of joy, happiness, and fulfillment. The solar card reminds you of confidence. This trust will be the light that shines in your relationship. Thanks to its appearance, you can be sure that your love relationships will reach a new level of connection and harmony. And most importantly, your intuition will lead you into your love relationships.

Tarot sun card traditionally represents success. The sun often brings news about weddings, births, financial results, celebrations, the completion of important projects, and joy. The sun represents a new perspective and clarity. A person achieved internal integrity when his unconscious and consciousness United.

As for the love life, The Sun is a positive sign. The sun indicates a period of celebration and happiness. If you are in a serious relationship, then this happiness will be shared between you and your partner. There will be new levels of mutual understanding and compassion. As for the love of Tarot data, the sun can refer to family affairs. In some cases, the sun may refer to pregnancy and/or the beginning of a new family.

For a man, the sun reminds you to get there. Now it's time to celebrate who you are. There's a good chance you'll meet someone new. If you have enjoyed one in the past, you may be ready to look for another significant one. In the love tarot, The Sun can mean a new relationship and often refers to the realization of desire.

Finally, The Sun Tarot card encourages you to become playful. Whether you're in a relationship or not, now is the time to enjoy life. Get ready to drain your inner Baby. The ultimate goal is to express yourself without self-awareness or fear. In love tarot readings, the sun serves as a reminder to always be your true self.

Traditional Tarot

The tradition of Tarot is estimated at more than five hundred years, with archetypal roots, which can be traced almost two thousand years. Traditional tarot gave way to modern methods of divination, but still remains a reservoir of ancient wisdom. Traditional tarot cards are the original source of modern playing cards.

The history and origin of the Tarot are not entirely clear. However, many theories support the belief about its origin from various places such as China, India, or Egypt. The oldest tarot cards that were found, however, dated back to the fifteenth century and were found in Spain, Italy, and France. According to historical evidence, traditionally, tarot cards were used as playing cards with pictures that showed living conditions, liberal arts, and virtues such as temperance and prudence. It is generally believed that, initially, tarot cards were not used as a means of divination.

Traditional tarot cards have been adapted to the current styles, and the Tarot Cards of the rider-Waite, the tarot card of Aquarius, the tarot card of Crowley Thoth, and the Tarot Card of Cagliostro are now considered to be the most basic and traditional tarot cards. These maps are designed based on historical maps and are considered an ideal option for beginners. Rider-Waite Tarot was designed in 1909 by artist Pamela Coleman Smith, according to specifications provided by Arthur Edward Waite. This pack contains seventy-eight cards with 56 smaller Arcane cards and 22 major mysterious cards. But the package has revolutionized traditional decks by assigning images to smaller mysterious cards. This deck is the most popular tarot deck in the world, which is preferred by beginners and advanced tarot students.

However, most tarot historians consider the entire tarot decks used in practice before the nineteenth century as historical bridges. Traditional tarot decks are considered strictly based on bridges, which prevailed at the time of Golden Dawn. Platinum A. E-mail. Waite and Pamela Coleman Smith are good examples of traditional tarot decks. These tarot decks further led to more popular board runners-Waite and deck Thoth.

Celtic Dragon Tarot

For the ancient Celts, the Dragon symbolized fertility or the creation of the Earth. They believed that a dragon formed the first cell born from the Earth and fertilized by the sky of wind and water. When the ancient Druids spoke of Celtic Dragons, they referred to dragon lines. These lines were considered places where most of the energetic, magical, and cosmic forces appeared on Earth and where their ritual meetings took place. They believed that dragons were creatures of a parallel world and, as such, sanctified these meeting places.

In mythology, King Arthur was overwhelmed by the dreams of dragons at the time of Mordred's conception and even before his own death. The Celts have long believed that when the King sees the Dragon, destruction will come to Earth. Still, it remains an important Celtic symbol depicted on the flag of Wales.

Tarot Dragon

Tarot cards of the Celtic Dragon have only been there for a few years. What makes it special, there are spells and meditations to accompany the bridge, which are intended to guide the reader through various exercises to invoke the energy of the Dragon and perform sacred visualization.

To illustrate this, each deck contains a spell for Prosperity. This means lighting a green and Golden candle. After they are placed on the altar with three specific cards, confirmation is repeated, and prosperity is welcomed.

Dragon tarot follows the same basic structure as traditional tarot cards. He has 78 cards, which are divided into four seeds are pentagrams, cups, swords, and wands. The cards correspond to wands with air and swords with fire. There are 22 major Arcane cards and 56 minor arcane cards.

The causes are represented as such.

Pentacles are given the sense of the Land Of Dragons involving elements of the earth, Northern energy, and physics

The cups have the meaning of water dragons and include elements of water, Western Energy and emotional

Swords stand behind fire dragons, and their corresponding elements are fire, south, and your energy.

Wands mean aerial Dragons with aerial, Oriental and mental elements

Small differences

There are some small changes in the names of the main Arcanes, and the names and numbers are displayed in Arabic numerals. Other changes are that The Hierophant will replace the High Priest, and chains will replace the devil. The formal ceremonial sectors of The Hierophant and the devil is not part of Celtic mythology these new representations of meaning.

Smaller bows use traditional outfits, but their corresponding elements are different. For example, wands are depicted as air instead of fire, and swords as fire instead of air.

The titles of the suit have not changed, and the cards of the court remain as king, queen, knight, and Page. It is worth noting that both sexes have changed; for example, a knight can be represented by a woman. Celtic does not discriminate against men and women, and it is common for men and women to work side by side. They went to war together, too. This aspect of Celtic tradition has been translated into these maps.

Changes in some photos are interesting and show that the magician is a woman. They also show that the High Priestess is active and dynamic. The women in these

Celtic Dragon Tarot Cards are portrayed as physically strong and powerful. Perhaps these representations are meant to mean what we know about the former Celtic Women.

Each card in the main Arcane has a full-size black and white image of each card and is accompanied by a keyword. Each card also receives a description, as well as a divine meaning, but there are no inverted meanings.

The creators of these Celtic tarot cards believe that the Dragon is dedicated to bringing radiant energy to life in the traditional tarot structure. Each image uses Dragons to reflect its meaning and uses backgrounds that reflect the Celtic history, culture, and symbols.

What makes this pack is excellent Celtic Dragon art on each card and on the back of each card is decorated with Celtic knot design.

A Tarot Spread and Unique Form of Tarot Reading

The Celtic spread of Tarot Cards is used for most of the data. It also refers to the unique form of Tarot and reading (but we'll talk about it later). Positions are numbers, and each number represents a specific context for each card.

They are as follows:

1. Current position (atmosphere in which the questioner is currently working)

2. Instantaneous influence (shows the nature of the influence or the obstacles that lie directly in front of it)

3. Purpose or Destiny (shows the purpose or destiny of the interviewer. It presents the best that can be achieved due to the existing circumstances)

4. Far into the past (shows great events and influences that existed in the past and are based on current events.)

5. Recent past events (shows recent events that affect the current location.)

6. Future influence (shows the sphere of influence that will come into being in the near future.)

7. Interviewer (shows the current location or interviewer's location. Try to put the question in the right point of view.)

8. Environmental factors (shows the influence of the interviewer on other people and events. It reveals trends and factors in relation to other people that can affect the partner.)

9. Inner emotions (they show the inner hopes and hidden emotions, desires, fears, and anxieties of the interviewer, including future thoughts.)

10. The final result (climax and results of all influences as revealed in the provided reading of the event and influences continue as stated.

Preservation of Celtic mythology

Few people realize that Celtic mythology is so fascinating and could be used on the side of the Tarot constructive path. Using the stories of Celtic mythology, we can gain greater depth and understanding of tarot reading. By interpreting these stories specifically, our unconscious minds allow them to become powerful tools to better understand our lives.

Celtic tarot cards were created as a way to restore the lost connection of Celtic mythology and Celtic art in the ancient wisdom of tarot cards. Combining the traditional meaning of tarot cards with popular characters from Celtic history, especially through the arturské tradition.

Celtic myth and legend, like tarot cards, come from a clear space and show us the portal that connects the spiritual world with our daily life. The typical art of Celtic Tarot, depicting the wonders of Celtic tradition and the wisdom of Tarot, combines to make this process a very pleasant experience.

Celtic Culture On The Brink Of Extinction

Its devoted followers strongly love pagan Celtic mythology. The world is probably very little of other cultures, which arouse as much interest as the Celtic people. However, over time, this culture has been obscured to the extent that it is suffocating and clear. The main contributors include Christianity, the Greek Zodiacs, and the Olympic Pantheon.

This unique version of the Tarot will be a great addition for those who practice the art of tarot, or for those who feel connected to the Celtic culture. Breast Art Maps is beautiful and provides a good way to help preserve Celtic history and tradition.

Tarot Symbolism and Meaning of the High Priestess Tarot Card

As for the symbolism of the Tarot, the card of the High Priestess is full of rich representative images and meanings. He is the embodiment of deep secrecy and secrecy. When she appears in the tarot reading, the High Priestess is a map of dreams, visions, and performances of all the secrets of the universe. It represents the intuitive female aspects of our media. As for development, he speaks of his inner voice and intuitive consciousness. It's an area of internal knowledge.

When reading the Tarot, the High Priestess is a female archetype. Unlike a magician who is active in nature, the High Priestess prefers passivity. It is associated with the unconscious, and its receptivity makes it an ideal female symbol. His receptive character allows him to explore the secrets and mysterious elements of the natural world.

The symbolism of Tarot number two: the tarot card of the High Priestess is the second card in the main Arcanes. Its connection with Number Two represents balance, harmony, and duality. In a tarot reading, the two often refer to the polarity, and if the card High

Priestess tarot number two refers to dualism found in the natural world and the psyche. The papacy represents a crossroads where two opposites meet. It has the ability to explore all Antipodes and use this energy to create something completely new.

The symbolism of the Tarot two pillars: in traditional tarot decks, the High Priestess is represented between two pillars, one black, and the other white. The pillars refer to the duality so often represented in the natural world: light and dark, night and day, birth and death, and positive and negative. Psychologically, both pillars relate to both male and female aspects of the psyche, as well as conscious and unconscious parts of the mind. Symbolically, this concerns her ability to plunge the High Priestess into the realm of the unconscious and carry her wisdom into conscious consciousness.

The symbolism of the tarot veil: behind the sitting priestess is a veil. The veil, a symbol of everything that remains invisible in the natural world, hides its hidden knowledge. The High Priestess serves as the guardian of secret wisdom. Its main purpose is to preserve everything that is considered sacred. When reading, the Tarot is a wise teacher and urges it to seek its own veil of rational thinking and look into their own unconscious wisdom.

The symbolism of the moon Tarot: in most tarot decks is the high priestess associated with the moon, which is usually represented by a crescent moon at his feet. The moon represents the female, emotional, unconscious, and intuitive elements of our psyche. It reminds us to rely on the soft light of the moon. This is the light of intuition. When reading the Tarot, the High Priestess presents our own inner knowledge. His connection with the Moon suggests that hidden knowledge can always be found in us.

The Moon also represents things that can remain invisible. The moon is a woman's night and often represents overshadowed aspects of the media. When reading the Tarot, the moon can be a symbol of the female mother, the inner child, and the influence of her subconscious.

The symbolism of the Tarot: on the knees of the priestess lies the role. In traditional tarot decks, the Scroll is associated with the Hebrew Torah. This concerns the need of the High Priestess to respect the Divine Laws of the natural world. It is also a scroll in which he records his memories. It represents all the knowledge and experience of the High Priestess. It serves as a container for mystery and mysterious knowledge, reflected in our world.

Discover the Meaning of the Chariot Tarot Card

The Chariot is the eighth card in the Order Of The Tarot game. Like the lover's card before, the Chariot also has a lot to do with the realm of emotions. However, it is important to note that the emotions involved are no longer in its pure and unlimited form. The car is about productivity and performance that occurs once you learn to control, channel, and tame your emotions and instincts. Only when you can control yourself Can you hope to control the world around you or any of the people in it.

The tank teaches us that the path to such mastery passes through the diligent self-discipline, which allows the use of a military symbol for the ideals that this card represents an incredibly appropriate. As well as the army promotes self-discipline and resilience through the difficult tactics so that new employees can better triumph under pressure, the car shows us the path to achievement and fulfillment through self-control and self-awareness. When we learn the lesson that you learn once and for all, we are not just a better survivor in the face of life's difficulties, but also more complete beings, ready for anything, what can life throw.

The traditional image of the tarot card of the tank depicts a royal male figure inside the tank itself. The vehicle itself is usually depicted as cartoons by two sphinxes of different colors, although there are many pictures of cars with traditional horses instead. Two sphinxes of different colors symbolize the opposite poles; positive and negative, dark and light, etc. The fact that the car driver successfully took advantage and used their innate power transfer from the place where they are, where they should be symbolizes the triumph of the human spirit over the challenge, adversity, instinct, and irrationality.

The image as a whole serves to remind us that while we are the people, we need our emotions, our driving force in the world, they are not productive forces, which may be if they are properly used and exploited. Instead of pain, anger, or other strong emotions and letting ourselves be consumed, we can channel them into productive activities that make us better.

When the Chariot appears in the spread of tarot cards, it usually means the presence of a situation where a similar control of emotions and instincts is needed.

The Quaker should not allow his energy to be wasted by self-pity, idleness, or fear. Instead, he should understand that he is asked to stand up, take control of himself for the better, and in the future, fight with the chin raised.

Printed in Great Britain
by Amazon